M000314314

Presented To:

_____

From:

_____

Date:

_____

# SUPERNATURAL
# ANOINTING

## OTHER BOOKS BY JULIA LOREN

*Shifting Shadows of Supernatural Experiences*

*Shifting Shadows of Supernatural Power*

AVAILABLE FROM DESTINY IMAGE PUBLISHERS

# SUPERNATURAL
# ANOINTING

A Manual for Increasing Your Anointing

# JULIA LOREN

© Copyright 2012–Julia Loren

All rights reserved. This book is protected by the copyright laws of the United States of America. This book may not be copied or reprinted for commercial gain or profit. The use of short quotations or occasional page copying for personal or group study is permitted and encouraged. Permission will be granted upon request. Unless otherwise identified, Scripture quotations are from the New International Version. HOLY BIBLE, NEW INTERNATIONAL VERSION®, Copyright © 1973, 1978, 1984 International Bible Society. Used by permission of Zondervan. All rights reserved. Scripture quotations marked WEB are taken from the World English Bible. Public Domain. Scripture quotations marked TNIV are taken from the HOLY BIBLE, TODAY'S NEW INTERNATIONAL VERSION®. Copyright © 2001, 2005 by Biblica®. Used by permission of Biblica®. All rights reserved worldwide. Scripture quotations marked NLT are taken from the Holy Bible, New Living Translation, copyright 1996, 2004. Used by permission of Tyndale House Publishers, Wheaton, Illinois 60189. All rights reserved. Scripture quotations marked KJV are taken from the King James Version. Public Domain.Please note that Destiny Image's publishing style capitalizes certain pronouns in Scripture that refer to the Father, Son, and Holy Spirit, and may differ from some publishers' styles. Take note that the name satan and related names are not capitalized. We choose not to acknowledge him, even to the point of violating grammatical rules.

DESTINY IMAGE® PUBLISHERS, INC.
P.O. Box 310, Shippensburg, PA 17257-0310

*"Promoting Inspired Lives."*

This book and all other Destiny Image, Revival Press, MercyPlace, Fresh Bread, Destiny Image Fiction, and Treasure House books are available at Christian bookstores and distributors worldwide.

For a U.S. bookstore nearest you, call 1-800-722-6774.
For more information on foreign distributors, call 717-532-3040.
Reach us on the Internet: www.destinyimage.com.

ISBN 13: 978-0-7684-4059-1
ISBN Ebook: 978-0-7684-8891-3

For Worldwide Distribution, Printed in the U.S.A.

1 2 3 4 5 6 7 8 9 10 11 / 15 14 13 12

# ENDORSEMENTS

With the wit of a sage, the research of a scholar, the pen of a scribe, and an adventure streak of a Holy Spirit Indiana Jones, Julia Loren brings many facets together when she writes. Through interviews of pioneers, teaching from Scripture, and testimonies of both modern-day mistakes and breakthroughs, *Supernatural Anointing* brings us a melting pot of understanding for the days in which we live. It is an honor to endorse the book you have in your hands. Blessings to you as you read, and a big thank you to Julia Loren for bringing us another contemporary masterpiece.

James W. Goll
Encounters Network • Prayer Storm • Compassion Acts
Author of *The Seer, The Lost Art of Intercession*
*The Coming Israel Awakening* and many more

You are on a spiritual journey to fulfill your destiny and calling. The anointing is our most precious possession in living a naturally supernatural life.

Julia Loren has compiled interviews of people who carry a strong anointing. My prayer is that Christ, the Anointed One, will fill you with fresh oil that will transform your life and the world.

Where the anointing flows, Christ is glorified.

Leif Hetland
President
Global Mission Awareness

With considerable depth, insight, research, and wisdom, Julia Loren has once again provided an incredible tool for the Body of Christ. Her book, *Supernatural Anointing,* will function like a blueprint to not only understanding God's dealings with His people in times past but also in the days ahead. Clearly, our generation will not experience the harvest as promised in Scripture without God's supernatural anointing. More than that, it is His Abiding Presence. The Kingdom principles outlined in the book that you now hold in your hand will certainly facilitate greater understanding of the anointing and position us to flourish in the supernatural realm as trustworthy stewards of His power and authority.

Paul Keith Davis
WhiteDove Ministries

I believe the Bride of Christ is in an hour of Awakening. We are being awakened from the nightmares of apathy, defeat, failure, and fear—we are being awakened in love—awakening to the Anointed One Himself! The Body of Christ is coming into a season of mighty power, faith, and love! In her book, *Supernatural Anointing,* Julia Loren describes how everyday believers can access the supernatural anointing of the Anointed One and release His character, nature, and miraculous healing power! These everyday believers may not be recognizable like the well-known names and faces of Christianity today, but they are known intimately by Jesus and have all of Heaven's backing! In the pages of this book, you will find wisdom on how to live and flow in the anointing, insight concerning the enemy's deceptive tactics on luring you out of the anointing, and even practical ministry advice on recovering from burnout! If you believe you're called to advance the Kingdom of Heaven in the earth and live a lifestyle of walking in the supernatural, this book is a must-read!

Jeff Jansen
Global Fire Ministries

# TABLE OF CONTENTS

Foreword................................................................13

Introduction.........................................................19

**Section I**    **Embracing the Anointing**................23

Chapter One    Awakening to the Anointed One.......27

Chapter Two    Facing the Winds of Worship............39

Chapter Three   Stepping Into Your Sacred Destiny.........57

**Section II**    **Shifting Shadows of Deception**.......73

Chapter Four    Aborting the Anointing......................77

Chapter Five    From Burning One to Burning Out.........99

Chapter Six    Restoring the Anointing.......................117

**Section III**      **Let the Anointing Flow**................................ 147

Chapter Seven   Releasing the Anointing in Everyday Life...... 151

Chapter Eight    From Ambassador's Anointing

                 to Apostolic Power........................................... 175

Chapter Nine     Your Future in God's Anointing...................... 209

                 About Julia Loren............................................ 221

# FOREWORD

Basically, I am a revivalist. If I were a hoarder, I would have to qualify on the basis of piggishness for life. Fill my house with life until it is overflowing! I live to receive, release, and retain life. I want all the life I can get; I want to give away all the life I can. Jesus came that we will have life, even life more abundantly. I don't do well with death. I don't do well with sickness and disease. In fact, I don't do well with any type of deficiency, be it spiritual, mental, physical, financial, and social. I am a revival junkie because I read my Bible. I am an awakening junkie. I am an anointing junkie. I will not be satisfied until I see the whole Church mobilized at every level in its Pentecostal (Acts 2) mandate in this generation.

Great revivals and awakenings have occurred over the centuries. People repeatedly ask, why in the space of a couple generations does a complete dissipation occur, the disappearance of revival? We haven't changed much since the Israelites' time when Joshua became leader.

Judges 2:7-11 speaks of those Israelites saying, *"who had seen all the great works of the Lord, that He did for Israel…and there arose another generation after them, which **knew not** the Lord, nor yet the works that He had done for Israel. And the children of Israel did evil in the sight of the Lord, and served Baalim"* (KJV).

Faith in God, anointings, ministry gifts, mantles, and mighty movings in the Holy Spirit cannot be transferred from generation to generation without new manifestations of the power of God as well as individual encounters. God is agitating us, stirring the pot, aggravating us, allowing us to remain desperately miserable until we begin to cry out for all that He has for us. And we will remain unsatisfied until we receive the fullness of what He longs for us to possess in this new era.

We are overdue for a great move of God. We are overdue for a revival that reaches farther than Toronto; Pensacola; Redding, California; Kansas City; Charlotte, North Carolina; and Mobile, Alabama. We are overdue for a brand-new thing, an awakening of cities, states, provinces, and nations that ends with a great turning back to God. We are overdue for a massive breaking out of the Kingdom of God. This is going to take an amazing encounter with God first on the part of individuals. Every revival or awakening that I have traced started with someone being overcome through an amazing encounter with God that changed his or her life.

Hah! But we are beginning to see little trickles, maybe even streams of the power of the Holy Spirit, the Kingdom of God, breaking out in places not only in America but also in Europe and other continents. There are nations that are being overtaken by God at this point in history.

I live in Michigan. When the recession of 2008 hit us, we were at the bottom of the barrel. We ranked #1 in the nation for unemployment, for financial devastation. A house in Detroit could be bought for a price cheaper than a car. The entire state was covered with gloom, despondency, despair, and hopelessness. We were riddled with corruption in Detroit. No one trusted the government, the business and economic sector, or even the schools. Faith in God hit an all-time low. Churches collapsed, some closed for good; buildings were foreclosed, and it felt like it was over. It was an incredible, horrific ending to an era of flush living. Yet that ending ushered in a new beginning.

What created that new beginning? It was a few people who still believed, who had for years believed that God could change a city and a state. It was leaders who had a calling from God and an anointing to take us somewhere we'd never been before. Somebody stood up and said, "We won't stop believing! The Bible is true. God can change a people; a city; a state." Now this state is on the verge of an awakening as well as a transformation.

The mayor of Detroit has opened up to the Church, expecting it to take a prominent position in changing the city. Several leaders of city government are believers in Jesus who are also Spirit-filled. Believers surround these governmental leaders and are speaking from the heart of God into key decisions as well as the direction of not only the city, but also the state. Our governor has attended a session on The Seven Mountains led by Lance Wallnau. Our lieutenant governor is a Spirit-filled believer. This April, 25,000 people filled Ford Field, home of the Detroit Lions, to pray for the city. This was after they had prayer-walked the city.

Our governor has stated that he has heard what God has said about Michigan and it will be the "turnaround state" that creates a new paradigm for the nation. He acknowledges the place of God in the transformation of this state.

What is all of this about? It's about one person here, one person there who heard the voice of God and began to move out under the direction that the Holy Spirit gave him or her. Because it was the Holy

Spirit, that person has an "anointing" from God to accomplish something, to do something, to release life that changes something.

We are living in a miraculous era, a time when we can't live without the amazing, life-giving release of the Kingdom of God. This is what this book is about! It's about the anointing; it's about hearing God; it's about specific people who learned to powerfully move out in specific giftings and anointings. It's about protecting the anointing so we don't fall, fail, or wear out unnecessarily. It's about who you and I are to be in this lifetime. It's about our joining hands with the generation above or below us and letting the fire of God ignite and join our hearts to change a city, a state, a nation—one person by one person by one person.

I am a radical, a radical lover of and believer in Jesus and His Word. Julia lays it all out here. Though she didn't express it this way, she is talking about the restoration of the New Testament Church in our generation, accomplishing the mandate that is on our plate.

The early Church was an amazing church. The devil had killed James in Acts 12. Now he thought he would take Peter out, the second of the three pillars (Peter, James, and John). If he could take the pillars out, he could stop the Church by demoralizing the followers through devastation and grief. However, there was a problem to his plan. He was dealing with real believers who had been baptized in the Holy Spirit and were bold. They knew they had an anointing and that prayer was powerful. Through their anointed praying in the Holy Spirit, Peter was miraculously delivered from prison in Acts 12. The early believers just plain believed in the miraculous power of God. They knew they were anointed.

Most of those early believers didn't change cities or nations through powerful preaching, prophetic direction, or apostolic power; but they took the anointing and calling they had and affected the lives of ordinary people as well as those of great leaders. Furthermore, they provided the believing furnace of fiery faith that ignited Peter, Paul, and others who did change entire cities and nations. The simplest of believers put the words of Jesus into practice, laying hands on the sick, casting out demons, speaking with new tongues, raising the dead. Today they would be coworkers with the Heidi Bakers of the world, the John Arnotts, Bill Johnsons, Chuck Pierces, Dutch Sheets, John Mulindes, Reinhard Bonnkes, Bill Hamons, David Yongghi Chos, and Benson Idahosas.

Shifting shadows of supernatural anointing! God is restoring a people who believe in the supernatural power of God. God is releasing His anointing to all who want Him and the power that accompanies those who believe in Him. He is raising up a generation who will do greater works than Jesus. This book will build your faith, create understanding, show you what the anointing looks like, help you to avoid pitfalls, and restore you to your God-ordained calling and anointing. It will ignite each generation to arise and be able to say what David said, *"The zeal of* [my Father's] *house hath eaten me up!"* (See Psalms 69:9).

Sit on the edge of your seat and fasten your seat belt as you walk with Julia Loren through this great book. This is a woman who has an insatiable hunger to see the ushering in of the Kingdom of God through ordinary people with radical faith; people who believe they are cutting-edge worldchangers because of the anointing that they have been given.

Read on....

BARBARA J. YODER
Senior Pastor and Lead Apostle
Shekinah Regional Equipping and Revival Center
Breakthrough Apostolic Ministries Network
Shekinah Leadership Institute
www.barbaraYODERblog.com; www.shekinahchurch.org

# INTRODUCTION

God is calling us forth to move in unprecedented power with the love that will move nations to awaken to who Jesus is, and to be a people who will walk in the stability that will enable us to disciple nations. That call initiated the *Shifting Shadows* series of books that I have written over the past few years. Around the world, many other voices are also sounding the call, some of whom I've interviewed for this book. We want to help position you to respond to the call, and for some, we look forward to your restoration of authority and anointing. You can attain the sacred destiny God has set apart for you and walk in greater authority and power than ever before.

We are all walking in a measure of supernatural anointing that I call the normal Christian life. Wherever we go, we know the Holy Spirit is with us and that when we walk into a room, His presence shifts the atmosphere. The emotions and chaos of the moment give way to His peace. Darkness flees as the light chases the shadows away. Joy infiltrates despair and raises hope. Healing happens. The earthly curtain parts, revealing the revelation of Heaven. Glory sweeps into a room and we talk with awe about these meetings for years to come. However, there is more.

For 33 years, I've been a Spirit-filled believer who lives a normal Christian life. Wherever I go, the Holy Spirit goes with me. We are inseparable. So are you and the Lord.

When I work in the worldly environments of my career path, I see the Holy Spirit at work through me. I've worked as a professional journalist and sought to impart the perspective and values of the Kingdom of God within an institution that operates under an antichrist spirit, an often hostile environment that eats Christians for lunch. And God came through. Then I trained as a professional counselor and worked with disaster response in the aftermath of natural disasters, consulted for the military in present and postwar family trauma, and counseled families. I've even trained church leadership groups and debriefed them in the aftermath of the tragedy of fallen leaders. God walked into every situation with me and I often walked out amazed by His goodness.

No matter if I have money coming in or not, whether I abase or abound, whether I work at secular employment to meet the bills or speak to crowds of believers and minister overtly in my prophetic calling, I see God move through me to shift the atmosphere and change lives. My stories are too numerous to list of His miraculous intervention in situations where He released supernatural authority and power to people who command the heights of international governments as well as serve the poor who dwell in remote villages on forgotten islands. Like you, I am an ordinary follower of Christ whose path has led me into strange and wonderful places. Like you, I know there is more of God's presence and power available in life and more of God to be known.

In my first book of this series, *Shifting Shadows of Supernatural Power,* I wrote about the convergence of the healing and prophetic movements and an emerging supernatural revivalist movement increasing its force as schools of supernatural ministry crop up all around the nation and the world. People recognize that the gifts of the Holy Spirit have always been available in fullness, not measure. We carry the fullness of the anointing and the gifts wherever we go. The gifts of the Spirit are integrated into our lives—at home, at church, in the supermarket, and at work. God leaks out of us and sometimes pours out on others like a sudden shower of love that brings a word of hope or a touch of His healing power. When we walk into a place, atmospheres shift, for God is in the room with us. We own that piece of real estate that our feet stand on. It is our little kingdom on earth to steward—our homes, our families, our communities, and our nation.

Learning to walk in the normal Christian life, full of His presence and authority and power, is part of appropriating our inheritance. We live from the position of being victorious rather than being victims. We step out in power rather than retreat in passivity. Even if we cannot, for some reason, leave our houses, we operate in the Spirit of power through intercession, knowing that our words are heard and angels move in response to God's authority as decreed through our prayers. Wherever we are, God is there.

The awakening to God's love and power, and our intentionally walking with awareness that His presence, authority, and power are always available to us, are the foundation to the next-generation anointing. It is increasing exponentially in our time. God is building up to something more.

## Exponential Increase Is Coming

As I prayed about the core message the Lord wanted me to impart through this book, I received a vision that was unlike any vision I have ever had. A math equation flashed before my eyes: **$Anointing^3$**. Immediately, I heard the voice of the Lord speak these words: ***"Exponential increase is coming as I raise the anointing to the third power."***

I don't think in terms of algebra and couldn't care less about math beyond calculating my taxes accurately. However, I recognized immediately what God was showing me. In algebra, when a number is cubed, it multiplies by itself three times. For instance, $2^3 = 2 \times 2 \times 2$, which amounts to 8. Also, the third power is the product of three equal terms.

Then the Lord directed me to read Second Timothy 1:7: *"For God did not give us a spirit of timidity, but a spirit of power, of love and of self-discipline."* Other translations speak of timidity as fear or cowardice and translate "self-discipline" as self-control, good judgment, sobriety, and wise discretion.

The next equation the Holy Spirit flashed before my eyes was this:

**Anointing$^3$ = *Power x Love x Sound Mind***

All three are equal and necessary components of the next-generation anointing. If you have the Holy Spirit, you have the power of God residing within you and others might take notice of the power of God within you and the gifts of God you wield. Multiply it with love and you have a force that others will receive—a double-portion anointing. Multiply that with the inner stability that evidences itself as the qualities of a leader—one who exercises self-control, good judgment, sobriety, and wise discretion, and you find yourself wielding an extraordinary increase of authority to move nations. Your power increases as a result of love and authority. Instead of you speaking the words of the Lord to others, the Lord backs up your words. He can trust you to speak under His authority. You find that you have grown from being a young believer who has learned to walk in Word and Spirit, to an ambassador moving with apostolic power.

No matter where you are at in your relationship with the Lord, welcome to this next leg of your journey into your sacred destiny!

JULIA LOREN

Section I

# EMBRACING THE ANOINTING

**Julia:**

Lord, what is the foundation of the anointing?

**Jesus:**

*Do you remember the day you first met Me? Or awakened to the idea of Me and found it so appealing that you struggled and pitched and rolled about like a ship in heavy seas, fighting the wind and the sea instead of running with it? I loved you then, and I love you still.*

*Do you remember when I opened your eyes to understand the Scripture and see Me in Word and Spirit? What amazement filled your mind as you "saw" with the eyes of your heart? I loved you then, and I love you still.*

*Do you remember surrendering to Me headfirst? Heart second? Life consecrated, baptized, and coming up out of the waters unsure that anything was different but knowing that you had reached the point of no return—that you were now Mine and I was yours, forever? I loved you then, and I love you still.*

*Do you remember how I stood patiently by, listening to your objections, taking on your rages against the injustice of life, letting you release your anger and pain and suffering, your hands beating against My heart as if you could break Me open and spill forth answers that would calm your heart and make every mystery of man's free will and My dealings with the world make sense? I loved you then, and I love you still.*

*Do you remember the first time you felt My embrace as a Father enfolding His beloved child, the smell of My robe, and the warmth of My expansive chest big enough to encompass the world but small enough to hold only you? I loved you then, and I love you still.*

*Do you remember how you felt when you were betrayed? So demolished by some man or woman that you felt you would never recover? And how I came to you, lifted you up when you were lost in your own pulsing blood, raging fear, and blinding pain, screaming wordlessly deep within yourself, in a place that lay beyond tears, in a place where only I could reach you? And one touch of My love, one word of knowledge, one healing vision, set you free? I loved you then, and I love you still.*

*Do you remember when satan stood before you and what happened next? I was so proud of you then, the way you overcame the enemy and did not give in that time. Oh, you may have think you failed other times but that time, I saw in you a reflection of Me and knew with a Father's joy that you would become more like Me than you ever thought possible. I loved you then, and I love you still.*

*Do you remember the first time you felt the overwhelming waterfall of My love raining down on you and knew that all would be well, and that I loved you then, and I always will?*

*Do you remember that My hand is on you to bless you and that you are not a failure? That you have not missed your calling? The very fact that you get up after a fall and start to walk toward Me again and again is an act of faith and trust in My faithfulness that speaks time after time that I will never cast away anyone who comes to Me and am one who forgives infinitely. Even in your times of doubt and shame, do you know that I loved you then and I love you still?*

*Do you remember your love for Me?*

*Because I remember My love for you—every moment of every day—I love you still.*

*And remembering our history together and being caught up in the awareness of My love is the foundation of all anointing.*

Chapter One

# AWAKENING TO THE ANOINTED ONE

The party in the bomb shelter was definitely getting out of hand. About a dozen volunteers from many countries joined those of us who were studying Hebrew in an Ulpan program on Kibbutz Yagur. A few Israelis straggled in and out. The alcohol flowed this New Year's Eve and the stereo volume crept upwards until every time the doors opened, rock and roll blasted into the surrounding area, cutting the peaceful night sleep of the kibbutzniks. The more we drank, the more boisterous and amorous we all became. The traditional midnight kiss on New Year's Eve went on and on, fueled by wine and beer. Finally, someone shut it down. It was time for bed. We all helped each other stumble back to our dorm rooms and promptly passed out.

I was 19, lost and wandering, trying to outrun the losses and pain in my life by traveling around the world. On my way to meet friends at an ashram in India, I stumbled into Israel instead and decided to spend the winter studying Hebrew in a community called a kibbutz, outside of Haifa, in the valley of Megiddo, at the base of Mount Carmel. Little did I know that my spirit was about to awaken to the greatest gift of all—the love of God, reaching out to me through the Jews, gathering all the fragmented splinters of my soul and solidifying me in Him. I was about to awaken to the anointing—the Christ—and it would alter the course of my life forever.

The morning after the party, the Ulpan Director, a grizzled ex-warrior who fought to establish Israel after the Holocaust, a short, stocky, and intimidating man, burst into my room. He was not pleased that we had all partied so hearty the night before. Pulling up a chair, he sat beside my bed where I was coming to in a haze of confusion, and he chastised me like a father correcting his daughter. I was shocked and defensive but, quiet. Suddenly, his face softened. He paused and said, "I think you need to get in touch with your God." Then he abruptly stood and walked out of the room.

Still dazed by the rude wake-up, I got dressed and headed for the dining room to see if I was too late for breakfast. I arrived at the same moment as a certain group of Holocaust survivors. Most kibbutzniks chose not to eat in the dining room when this particular group of Holocaust survivors entered—for good reason. They suffered from postwar psychosis; their minds had snapped. They shuffled in, clearly unaware of their surroundings, having survived the Holocaust only to shatter into a postwar psychosis from which they would never recover.

One woman, led by an attendant to the dining room table, shuffled up to her chair, her head snapping left to right, her eyes vacant. She sat down, staring straight ahead until the attendant brought her a plate of food. The woman leaned forward, her hands guarding her plate. As she rapidly shoveled the food into her mouth, her eyes kept vigil, snapping like a metronome from left to right, lest someone try to steal her food. Abruptly, she pushed her plate away and stood up, eyes wide open with fear, hopping sideways, from one foot to the other until the attendant led her away long before the others had finished eating.

My appetite left. I decided to go for a walk.

As I walked out the door, I flashed on the image of another Israeli Holocaust survivor I had seen while visiting a different kibbutz. He impressed me so much that I will never forget him. He stood near a coffeepot chatting with other kibbutzniks. I could tell from the way the others approached that they held him in high regard. This man radiated love and light and joy like no one I had ever seen before. Laughing at something the men shared, the man turned to pour himself a cup of coffee, exposing his forearm and revealing the crudely tattooed numbers that had seared his flesh but left his spirit soaring. This was the first God-filled man I had ever seen. I was in awe of the light and joyful, humble authority that radiated from him.

What was the difference between the man and this woman? Both survived unspeakable Nazi terror. Only one chose to leave the past behind and enter into the appointed times of feasting and celebration. Only one chose life. And to fully embrace life, he must have dealt with his past. I imagine that he grieved the loss of many family members, faced the loss of his youth, watched men die, and no doubt killed a few himself as he fought to establish a homeland. Yet he pushed through the grief, forgave his enemies, and forgave himself. Light stole the darkness from his heart. Joy conquered the pain. And he danced the folk dances of his day that were based on the psalms, and laughed and celebrated life—more and more every year.

I realized that somewhere along the way this man had encountered God. He radiated God. Somewhere in his journey, he received the abundant grace of the Lord who delights to reveal Himself, to reveal His nature. This man felt the touch of God and it was so healing, so delightful, that he was forever captivated by God's love and chose to live life with God. He was fully awake. And fully alive.

Who was this God who revealed Himself to Jew and Gentile? Who released such an awakening of someone's spirit that he could overcome all the pain of the past and come into a sense of personal destiny and anointing to build a future not just for one's self, but to establish a nation? Although I did not understand it then, I had a sense that the God whom the Ulpan Director suggested I get in touch with was his God, too, and that my sojourn in Israel was central to understanding Jesus. And clearly, we all need to be filled with God, His anointing, just to survive life.

Even at the young age of 19, I had experienced tremendous pain and loss and degradation. But it was nothing like what I saw etched on the skin of many in Israel. I knew that I didn't want to end up like the gathering of survivors at the table who were still lost in the hell of their past. I wanted what that God-filled man had. I was waking up.

As I walked toward the Pardess—the grapefruit orchard—one of the other Ulpan students joined me. She was a Jewish girl my age who was also from the States. We laughed and talked about the party as we walked along the dirt roads at the base of the mountain that seemed to grow straight up from where we stood. Suddenly, she looked up and pointed toward the unseen mountain peak and said, "Up there is where Elijah slew the prophets of Baal."

"Really?" I responded. "Was that in the Six-Day War? I didn't know the Syrians came down this far."

Stunned by my ignorance, she patiently explained who Elijah was and told me about his battle against Baal worship. I was intrigued. On the way back from our walk, she stopped off at her room and brought out a small Bible. Handing it to me she said, "Here, as you travel around, read this. It has a New Testament you may be interested in. I bought it for use as a historical guidebook and used it while traveling around Israel before I started the Ulpan program."

So the awakening had begun that day with two secular Jews leading me into the realization that I needed to get in touch with my God and giving me the means to begin. I assumed that this God was Jesus. And what better way to get to know Him than by walking around Israel, getting to know His people, walking where He walked, reading passages of His teachings in this historical book while standing near the same spot where He originally spoke the words. It was the beginning of learning about the Anointed One, Christ. That day also gave me the inkling that we, Jews and Christians, were mysteriously bound together in history and in spirit—past and present and forever.

It wasn't long after reading passages of the book that I got on my knees in my little dorm room and prayed a salvation prayer that was more like a challenge: "God, You have got to change my life."

And instantly, my life changed. I felt more solid and less weak when I stood up from that prayer. My appetite to read the whole book consumed all my spare time. I came to realize that I could now call myself a believer...a follower of Christ...a Christian.

After about a month, I asked God if there were any other Christians living in the country. It was 1979. Jewish believers remained hidden under threat of constant persecution. I knew there were some churches in Haifa, but I wasn't sure where to go. So I asked Him to lead me. A week later, I found myself in Jerusalem meeting another Christian my age who told me to try the meetings held in a youth hostel in Haifa. So I went the next Friday night and stayed the night as the busses had stopped running for Shabbat, the Jewish Sabbath.

About 20 people crowded into a room and began to worship joyfully, exuberantly, flowing from English to Hebrew to some other languages I couldn't decipher as they worshiped. I felt overwhelmed but saw that their joy was genuine. I decided that I would come back the following week and, if they were still that happy, I would ask them what they were on. I wanted whatever happy pill they were taking.

The next week, they were still happy. I asked. And they told me about the infilling of the Holy Spirit, gave me a concordance and some books, and sent me home to investigate the matter.

The following week, I asked them to pray for me. Immediately, I felt this tingling from my head to my feet, a giddy joy rising within me like little champagne bubbles that burst forth in fits of laughter. Love saturated my entire being. I had awakened to His love.

Experiencing the love of Jesus is the great awakening. Do you remember your great awakening? It is the foundation of all anointing.

During the weeks following that experience, I felt like my feet never touched ground. I was so full of His Spirit and joy. More than that, I realized that the eyes of my spirit had opened. I no longer saw just a person standing nearby. I no longer saw just buildings and sky and the Sea of Galilee, or the sands of the Mediterranean, or the sights and smells of Haifa's deep-fried falafels, huge sesame-studded bagels, and sizzling lamb roasting on street-side spits. I saw angels and demons coming and going in the air and on people, and I somehow discerned what they were up to.

I would sit at a bus stop and receive words of knowledge about people and start up conversations that began with them wondering how I knew what I knew about them. I didn't know how I knew. So I would go back to my room and ask God, "Where is that in Your Book?" And the Holy Spirit would teach me that the anointing was an anointing of power for the purpose of telling the world about Him.

*But you will receive power when the Holy Spirit comes on you; and you will be My witnesses in Jerusalem, and in all Judea and Samaria, and to the ends of the earth* (Acts 1:8).

The pattern of my spiritual and devotional life had been set. I would go to church and get filled up and give it all away during the week. I still do. And the Holy Spirit would always teach me if I sat down to inquire. He still does.

I was learning about the anointing directly from the Holy Spirit— the One whom I learned to trust as His Word backed my experiences.

*As for you, the anointing you received from Him remains in you, and you do not need anyone to teach you. But as His anointing teaches you about all things and as that anointing is real, not counterfeit— just as it has taught you, remain in Him (1 John 2:27).*

The awakening had begun. And I thought that this experiential knowledge of God's love, this joy, this ability to know what people were thinking and where they had been, this seeing of angels and demons and knowing how to pray, this sense that God would heal anyone I prayed for because He is a good God, the warnings of impending danger and how to get out of the way by avoiding a bus that was carrying a bomb in a basket, or sidestep the wrath of a radical Jew or Muslim, was the essence of the normal Christian life. The supernatural was meant to be super-normal.

God's desire has always been that we would awaken to His love and power, that our broken hearts would find all that we need in Him. But still so many Christians have no experience of awakening to His love or healing presence in their lives. Others, who once walked in the anointing, have turned aside, leaving their heart encounters with the Holy Spirit to retreat into their minds, or jobs, or troubles of this world. It is time to awaken, once again, to the anointing.

What does an awakened man, woman, or child look like? What does a church look like that is fully awake to God's anointing? Luke, my favorite Gospel author, gives us a few hints about how God awakens us. No matter how "old" you are in the Lord, remembering your first encounters, your first love, will restore even more of the anointing than you ever thought possible. And, particularly if you are an old believer, remembering your early days will help you to reconnect with unbelievers. For the anointing is, first of all, an anointing of love. Secondly, it is an anointing of power to be His witness in the earth. If you have lost sight of one or the other, you'd best step into a new awakening.

The awakened heart knows, somehow, that Jesus will receive the most broken of sinners. One woman in particular pushed past the fear, barged into a good-old-boys' meeting, and unashamedly had eyes only for Jesus. The awakened woman or man only has eyes for Jesus.

> When one of the Pharisees invited Jesus to have dinner with him, He went to the Pharisee's house and reclined at the table. A woman in that town who lived a sinful life learned that Jesus was eating at the Pharisee's house, so she came there with an alabaster jar of perfume. As she stood behind Him at His feet weeping, she began to wet His feet with her tears. Then she wiped them with her hair, kissed them and poured perfume on them (Luke 7:36-38 TNIV).

The woman only saw Jesus. Her tears expressed a heart of worship that no words could express. She anointed Him and ministered to Him, for one glance of His eyes transformed her life. She bowed low out of reverent awe and love, not even thinking about what others thought about her. Her heart was awakened by love and her automatic response was worship.

A couple of men, who had apparently been followers of Jesus but did not know Him, discovered their hearts awakening and burning within them, as they shifted from thinking about Jesus as a prophet to knowing Him as God. Suddenly, there was no more overfamiliarity or unfamiliarity. He had risen in their hearts and they woke up as God opened their minds to understand the Scriptures. First they had a head encounter where they logically worked out of the identity of Jesus. Then they had the heart encounter that awakened their hearts to know Him. Many believers know Him in their heads, but the awakening of their hearts is an awakening of worship that releases power.

*He said to them, "How foolish you are, and how slow of heart to believe all that the prophets have spoken! Did not the Christ have to suffer these things and then enter His glory?" And beginning with Moses and all the Prophets, He explained to them what was said in all the Scriptures concerning Himself.*

*As they approached the village to which they were going, Jesus acted as if He were going farther. But they urged Him strongly, "Stay with us, for it is nearly evening; the day is almost over." So He went in to stay with them.*

*When He was at the table with them, He took bread, gave thanks, broke it and began to give it to them. Then their eyes were opened and they recognized Him, and He disappeared from their sight. They asked each other, "Were not our hearts burning within us while He talked with us on the road and opened the Scriptures to us?"* (Luke 24:25-32 TNIV)

Their eyes were opened—they were awakened as they took communion with Jesus. They suddenly experienced a personal knowledge of the intimacy of Jesus and the meaning of communion—the full meaning of His blood shed and His suffering for them. Their hearts were burning because they were in the presence of the Anointed One.

They remembered Him—not just in the human body that He inhabited. They remembered Him in Spirit and the sensation of their hearts burning. It was a sensation they remembered from when they sat and listened to Jesus long before He was crucified. His words made their hearts feel strangely warmed. And that warmth flooded through them, causing them to recognize the presence of Jesus. They missed understanding the fullness of Christ when they walked with Him. But now, the eyes of their understanding were open and they recognized Him. They became fully awake.

Peter, James, and John were the only disciples to fully awaken to the glory of God. Their awakening led them to become the leaders of the early Church, moving with authority and power never before seen. Jesus had invited them to go away for a little prayer time. Apparently, they stood at a little distance from Jesus, giving one another space to pray individually rather than corporately, probably bored that they were on yet another prayer journey with Jesus, stuck on a mountain top all day long, the sun lulling them to sleep. Suddenly:

> *As He was praying, the appearance of His face changed, and His clothes became as bright as a flash of lightning. Two men, Moses and Elijah, appeared in glorious splendor, talking with Jesus. They spoke about His departure, which He was about to bring to fulfillment at Jerusalem. Peter and his companions were very sleepy, but when they became fully awake, they saw His glory and the two men standing with Him* (Luke 9:29-32).

If you have fallen into a drowsy state of only occasionally acknowledging the presence of Jesus, it is time to wake up. It is time to come back to your first love. Remember the early days when you awoke to the realization that Jesus is alive and had the first encounter with His love. That great awakening is yours, once again. The Lord is inviting you, too, to witness the transfiguration of not only Himself, but also of His Church. The appearance of your face will change as the glory of God flashes upon you. The cloud of His presence will envelop you as you have an encounter with God. Suddenly, you will discover who He is and who you are to Him, once again. You will realize that you are filled with His power and authority, commissioned to take it out to the world, reenvisioned to a specific calling or task. It is time to wake up! Fill your lamp with oil and realize that the Lord desires you. The Lord has need of you. Your reawakening will result in your reanointing.

Listen. He is saying this to you:

> **Do you remember the day you first met Me? Or awakened to the idea of Me and found it so appealing that you struggled and pitched and rolled about like a ship in heavy seas,**

*fighting the wind and the sea instead of running with it? I loved you then, and I love you still.*

*Do you remember when I opened your eyes to understand the Scripture and see Me in Word and Spirit? What amazement filled your mind as you "saw" with the eyes of your heart? I loved you then, and I love you still.*

*Do you remember surrendering to Me headfirst? Heart second? Life consecrated, baptized, and coming up out of the waters unsure that anything was different but knowing that you had reached the point of no return—that you were now Mine and I was yours, forever? I loved you then, and I love you still.*

*Do you remember your love for Me?*

*Because I remember My love for you—every moment of every day—I love you still.*

*And remembering our history together and being caught up in the awareness of My love is the foundation of all anointing.*

Chapter Two

# FACING THE WINDS OF WORSHIP

The crowd stepped out of their seats, some moving to the front of the auditorium that housed the Toronto Christian Fellowship. Others, like me, stepped off to the right side, into the wide expanse where I positioned myself beneath an empty cross that hung low on the wall.

Contagious joy swept through the room as Georgian Banov[1] fiddled us into dancing. Even the feet of the most stoic European could not help but shuffle. Joy has a way of moving your body before your mind can shut it down. We shuffled, hopped, danced, and let Georgian lead us along like the pied piper leading children along leading along a path children who cared not where they were going. We were swept along into the path of least resistance and went up the Kingdom road.

Suddenly, Georgian transitioned us from joy to holy awe in a way that no musician could have done. It was supernatural. The thin veil that keeps us from being fully awakened to the reality of the spiritual Kingdom surrounding us, opened. We all got a glimpse behind the curtain.

Immediately, I went into a vision—no, I became a vision. I became Mary kneeling at the foot of the cross, weeping inconsolably because Jesus had been taken away. The vision lasted just a few minutes and the presence of God lifted. When I lifted my head and started to come up from my knees, I noticed an odd sight. The whole side of the room, perhaps 50 or so people, had fallen like matchsticks scattered out of a box. We had worshiped our way out of the earthly room, and somewhere along the road, we passed through an invisible barrier and entered the Kingdom of God.

One moment we were in a room full of worshipers. The next moment, our faces were full on in the winds of the Spirit that blow in on the sounds of worship. And in that Kingdom, visions happen, healing happens, God meets you, and you are transformed in His presence. Every encounter with God changes us on a deeply spiritual level. Just being in the atmosphere of His presence expands our spirit and increases our ability to see and to walk in two worlds—the earthly realm and the spiritual realm surrounding us.

The awakening is not only about knowing the anointing of love and power; it is the awakening to worship. Both head and heart are alive and awake to Him when they fully connect with God in worship. The awakened man or woman knows this. The awakened Church lives this out and takes it out to the world.

Years after the Toronto worship experience, I found myself attending a Randy Clark conference in Seattle with Leif Hetland, Dennis Balcomb, and others. Davi Silva and his band from Brazil led worship. One night the worship released a warlike sound that swept the worshipers up and into the sound of Heaven invading earth forcefully, intentionally. Fire touched down here and there on the heads of others. Fire swept along the curtains near the stage. Many in the room caught the images of flames on camera. For a brief moment of grace, the fire burned out the impurities within us.

All that night, I was enabled to see the reality of what God was doing. Angels moved in. I saw the most amazingly colorful rings of light surrounding one of the speakers like giant, electrified Hula-hoops®, like wheels within the wheels of divine protection, and I realized how one anointed man could stand before hostile masses of Muslims bent on killing him and stop them in their tracks. Even if their eyes could not see, their spirits would be arrested by the power surrounding him, protecting him like a force field. I saw what was contained in that zone of power around him. It must have been the same zone of power people perceived around Jesus. Although they could not see it with their natural eyes, some knew that if they could just reach into it, just touch the hem of His garment, they would be healed. The atmosphere of worship opens our eyes to see the unseen reality of Heaven on earth.

Every revival in history has seen worship leaders skillfully, and supernaturally at times, transition the people into a great awakening to His presence, His love, and His power. During this season in Church history, we are seeing worship emerge in such a way that we are going beyond the sense of the Holy Spirit coming in the wind, beyond the intoxicating feelings of new wine, and beyond the fire. We are coming into a time when corporate worship will target individuals to be anointed with oil—the empowering needed to accomplish their sacred destinies and accomplish the tasks set before them by the Lord. Many people believe that the next great awakening will become the great empowering of the Church; and worship will lead us into it and sustain us as we take it out into our sacred destinies.

All over the world anointed worship has opened the heavens for revival. Hillsong music awakened the nation of Australia much in the way that Maranatha Music of Calvary Chapel fame and Vineyard

Music awakened the Church in America. Today we see anointed young worship leaders leading us higher into revelation of God's love and motivation to carry His love into the world. Some are connected to specific streams and churches like the International House of Prayer, Jesus Culture, Christ for the Nations, and many large churches spread throughout the nation. Other musicians are independent but their worship anointing works in conjunction with itinerant ministers and paves the way for a greater release of Word and Spirit for those who attend. Some worship leaders, like Roy Fields, have carried the anointing to break open the heavens and unleash an outpouring in specific cities like the Lakeland Outpouring of recent years. There are too many independent worship leaders to list by name, and because there are so many, we are seeing a purity emerge in worship. The ones who focus on the Lord rather than on fame and finances seem to be the ones carrying the most anointing.

Let's take a look at how worship leaders create and maintain an atmosphere where the finger of God touches the hearts of people so that no one is ever the same. As you read the comments of Carl Tuttle, Danny Steyne, and Ray Hughes, you will begin to understand how the Lord has been leading the Western Church, specifically the American Church, into greater revelation of His presence and His heart. You will also catch a glimpse of where we are going from here.

Throughout my life, worship has always drawn me right into the heart of Jesus. That connection releases whatever I need for life, and even more to give away. Years after leaving Israel and finishing college, I found myself drawn to the Vineyard Christian Fellowship pastored by John Wimber, one of the founding members of the music group called The Righteous Brothers. He was the only pastor I had ever heard who talked about some of the same things that I had experienced in the supernatural, particularly as it relates to the gifts of the Holy Spirit. It was through his ministry that I realized how anointed worship carries us into the Anointing Himself and enables us to carry more of His anointing into everyday life.

Carl Tuttle[2] was one of the key worship leaders at the Anaheim Vineyard Christian Fellowship at the time I was there from 1980–1985. The anointing for worship and healing on John Wimber's life, and on the key worship leaders in the house, enabled many to connect with God and receive the healing and power they needed. But we not only received it; we gave it away. The anointing of revelation and healing begged to be released. The more we gave it away, the more we received. It kept us from becoming too self-focused and more solid in the realization that the anointing, the empowering that enabled us to release the gifts of the Spirit, was for others. Worship was, and will always be, central to experiencing the anointing. Worship in the Vineyard Movement paved the way for the healing gifts to flow and launched a renewal movement that swept across many mainstream churches.

I asked Carl about the anointing for worship during the days after the Jesus People move of God in the 1970s when the new anointing for worship was more fully embraced by many churches around the world who shed the old ways and old songs for the new. Most specifically, I asked Carl what increases the anointing. What follows is an excerpt from my interview.[3]

## Can you give me an example of a true anointing to lead worship?

I haven't gotten all that figured out; I think there is a whole spectrum of people who are anointed. I mean there are people like myself who write by inspiration. I'm not a Graham Kendrick who practices a song, and works on it, and develops it over a period of time. Most of the songs I've written just come to me and I write them down. I sing them and there they are. I watch people like Danny Clark who, in the early days of his leading worship, did not have the strong anointing that he has now. But now, when he leads worship I am just devastated because God comes. It's just a remarkable thing.

The thing I think that characterizes "the anointed worship leader," is that they are a worshiper themselves. If you watch Lori Barnett lead worship, she is fully engaged with God as she leads worship. Eddy Espinosa, the weeping worship leader [who also led worship at Anaheim Vineyard]—his heart is so tender before the Lord, and when he leads worship you can tell he is fully engaged and models a beautiful thing.

**And do you think that engagement with the Lord creates a breakthrough for those who are listening or are entering in themselves?**

Yeah, absolutely. I think it helps. If you've got somebody up there who is performing and trying to make themselves the center of attention, that certainly gets in the way of the people being able to engage in worship.

**It seems like John Wimber of the Vineyard movement really broke open anointed worship for the rest of the nation after the Jesus People days brought in a freedom of expression.**

I know that John and Carol recognized it very early on. As it grew, they were very clear that this thing was going to go around the world. I'm thinking, *You've got to be kidding. We've got a hundred people here who are a ragtag group at best, and this is going to go around the world?*

I remember many years later, I couldn't sleep one night so I was channel-surfing and all of a sudden I hear the song "Breathe" playing. I look and Michael W. Smith is at a piano, and as the camera pans back, I see that they are in the White House with George Bush and Condoleezza Rice. He's leading worship there. And I remembered what Carol had said. There wasn't this system in place like there is now—a whole worship industry. I don't even know how it took off and had a life of its own and stuff went around the world. Part of it, I think, was the simplicity of it all.

**I remember how simple some of the worship songs were, and it just brought us closer into the presence of the Lord. The most anointed worship songs are simple, from the heart, and to the Lord.**

If you look at the most popular worship songs based on the CCLI [Christian Copyright Licensing International] listings, the vast majority of them are the ones that are transferrable and accessible to the public. It's not that more complex songs aren't as great; they are just not as easily transferrable. The average church is 60 people, and you've got a very limited pool to draw from in terms of musicians and stuff. So things that people need to sink their teeth into or wrap their arms around need to be simple. It certainly helps.

**When you were first starting off a worship movement and the Vineyard was becoming popular, what was it that increased the anointing?**

Well, I think we took God really seriously. He showed up. We were gathering together out of a hunger for Him, out of a desire to connect with God somehow. And I remember really clearly in one of the gatherings, God's presence being there. He met us there and that became really central to us then— that He remained the focus. So we took that sense that God would move among us really seriously. We just didn't take ourselves very seriously. We made God's presence a major priority. I think prior to that, that—this was 1976 through 1977—I don't think there were very many places in Southern California or maybe the nation and around the world, that were dedicating 45 minutes of their service time to worship. There's one recording of a Sunday night when the church was located in the gymnasium where I did 17 songs.

## And what was the reaction to prolonged worship sets that focused on God's presence?

Oh, the people were engaged the whole time. I mean fully engaged. And then John would stand up and he'd talk and then we would have ministry time and it was just remarkable. There was just a real flow of what we did, very seamless, and very, very God-centered. The songs weren't about us and they weren't even about God as much as they were expressions of our hearts to God. Like the song "I Love You, Lord." It was an expression of love to God; our songs were prayers.

## I remember singing "I Love You, Lord," and my heart would just break, not because of my love for the Lord, but my own understanding of my lack of love for the Lord. That led me to ask for more ability to love Him, and ministry just happened; it was amazing. The simplicity helped us all engage in prayer as we were worshiping.

And He was the focus. There was no cheerleading, there was no grandstanding, there was no drawing attention to yourself. Our goal was to stay out of the way. Obviously, we had to play and we did as good a job as we could do. Obviously, John was a great musician. We did as well as we could do but we tried to stay out of the way of whatever God was doing and let Him be responsible for what was happening in the hearts and lives of people.

So I never said, or rarely said, everyone stand or everyone lift their hands or everyone clap or anything. I never did that sort of instruction. I always felt like that was a phony Holy Spirit. There would be one person on their knees and another person with their hands in the air and another person sitting in quietness before the Lord and so we just felt like it was important that the Holy Spirit orchestrate what took place during worship and it not be directed so much by us.

**When I see people in worship today, I see some of the people fully engaged and most of the people not. And the further the people are away from the platform, the less engaged they are. How do you get the whole room into the same place of engagement with the Lord?**

I don't know. In the worship conferences–and it doesn't matter if you're in the front row or the back row—people are there for that very purpose and people sit there engaged the whole day. Church can be different from a conference and personally I think it needs to be different. I think people enter in whatever level of faith they are at.

I'm from Southern California and I think of it like going to Newport Beach. You know you can drive up to the parking lot and you can sit; you can look out at the ocean at the people on the sand; or you can get out of the car and sit on the wall. Or you can get on the sand and lay out; or you can put your feet in the water; or you can dive all the way in. So you could have five different experiences or more and all are at the same beach. I think church is like that; there are people that are just ready to dive in and there are people that are going to sit in their cars with their windows rolled up and observe. So I kind of leave that up to the Holy Spirit to draw people in, as they are ready.

## You just don't manipulate people.

You just don't. Let God be God. We do our little part and let Him be God. I don't like things that are manipulated or are contrived. It's just really fun to see what Holy Spirit does in the midst of a group of people, and to know that it has nothing to do with us. I just got a letter from a gal who was in a conference we did in 1984, 26 years ago, telling me that during our meetings at Western Central Hall in London, God met her.

I remember really clearly we just led worship, and in quietness the Spirit of God moved throughout the room. Nobody said anything, nobody did anything, and nobody encouraged anything. I remember this scream, and in the midst of that she was delivered. And 26 years later this lady has a testimony of a transformed and changed life because God sovereignly met her and delivered her in that place. Nobody claimed to have anything to do with it. We were all just like observers. When she wrote me, I remembered exactly what she was talking about. I love that stuff.

## So what are the top three things you say that kill the anointing for worship or for any kind of ministry?

Pride would probably be number one of the list. I think it hurt Saul really bad. I think pride is the opposite of humility and so it just undermines what God is doing. Along with that, just being egocentric. I remember one night we were in the gymnasium at the end of worship. It was just quiet. And in our particular deal, you would notice it would be really calm and at that time somebody would prophesy. But John went to the microphone and said, "Let's just be still before the Lord," meaning don't anybody prophesy. Well, all of the sudden this guy started prophesying and I mean loud, in a very forceful voice, and I thought *Oh boy*.

John said, "I said, 'Let's be still before the Lord.'"

And the guy kept going.

John said, "Let the prophet be silent."

The guy kept going. Then I heard over to my right, where John was sitting at the keyboard, this groan coming from John. The prophecy stopped, and John spoke into the microphone and said, "Lord, I'm sorry. I didn't know You wanted to speak."

Most pastors that I've seen would've needed the person to know, right then and there, who was in control. If he said don't prophesy and you prophesied then you are in big trouble. But John wasn't driven by his ego in that setting so he submitted and said, "Oops, I blew it."

So I think pride and ego can undermine what God is doing. If it has to be about us, and our gifts, and what we bring, then I think that really undermines us. I also think a lack of openness kills the anointing. A lot of churches are so planned out—precisely 17 minutes of worship, and 22 minutes of the message, and 90 seconds of this—and there's no space, there's no room for anything to happen. So I think we can plan God right out of our meetings. I think that is some people's intent. I don't think they are comfortable with the Holy Spirit.

Wimber's worship influence and Calvary Chapel's worship influence broke open an intimacy that awakened a generation. But that was a generation ago. Where are we going now? Are we moving from grace to grace, from glory to glory, from old anointing to something new? I believe that we are in a transitional state forming the bridge into the new outpouring of God. What do I base this belief on? Absolutely nothing concrete. Just a sense from what I see and hear as time goes by: We are making quantum leaps into the future in every art form and industry. Nations are in upheaval. The earth groans and kicks back at the load on its back, and the winds and weather patterns and wars and rumors of wars are speaking about worldwide transformation. We stand at the brink. And to survive, we need God, as well as an ever-increasing anointing on worship. This will awaken unbelievers and release a quickening anointing of faith that will enable us to become comfortable with bringing Heaven to earth; with making the unseen, seen; and with releasing hope and peace in the midst of the great shaking going on in the world.

One man articulates what this transitional anointing of worship looks like. It is characterized by freedom and enables believers to not only connect with God in their hearts, but also to see Him more clearly as revelation pours out in visions, in healings and miracles, and in manifestations of signs and wonders.

Danny Steyne leads Mountain of Worship (MOW),[3] a congregation of revelatory worshipers in South Carolina that has spawned like-minded regional centers of worship around the world. In a sense, Danny is an apostolic leader who, because he has also been a worship leader for many years, is releasing a transitional anointing for worship characterized by total freedom and love. In this atmosphere of free worship, people begin to see visions; miracles happen; healings, signs, and wonders occur; and most importantly, people connect with God more intimately and more joyfully than they ever thought possible in "church."

Danny is definitely stretching the limits of the anointing to worship. Everyone I have talked to who has attended a conference at MOW met God in a powerful way, interacting with Him in the middle of worship—not at the end when an altar call may or may not have spoken to them.

For many mature believers, who have the Word so ingrained in them through years of attending church and listening to sermons, worship is what their hearts crave—not more sermons. They come away so full of God (who quickened healing, or the Word, or fresh vision in them) that they could not help but pass Him along to others.

In the following interview, I asked Danny about his views on worship and the anointing, and about what he wants to accomplish through them.

## What is this anointing for worship that you are imparting to others?

I've been doing worship since the 1980s. We have a number of leaders who know how to bring worship in a sense of carrying people to the throne, which is where the anointing flows from. I believe we are supposed to worship in Heaven over the earth. We've got to get there as quick as we can.

I've been to Heaven through visions, and seen that Heaven is not linear; it is multifaceted. Everything is happening at the same time. And if we are worshiping from the throne room, everything is happening all at once for people. It's not just people loving God; it is [also people] loving each other. By the end of our conferences, people are very much in love with God and gaga over each other as well. Our heart is to bring people into the atmosphere of Heaven, not just sing songs to God.

When I travel, I usually take a worship leader with me who will work with the band, and by the second day they will come into that place. It is equipping people and letting them know that it is OK to move freely in worship, in whatever expression the Lord is leading. What we have released is freedom in worship. It is starting to be released all over the place. Even in other movements. Now, it seems, the Lord is taking us even further than that because of what the Lord wants to pull us into, something that the Church hasn't touched yet.

## What do you think that looks like?

You can watch on YouTube a man coming out of wheelchair when kids prayed for him in the middle of worship. Those kinds of things are happening. I see something happening in the atmosphere in worship that is much more complete than simply a worship time. Many times, almost everybody has been very involved. Some are fully engaged because the Lord is so fully present that they can't move. People are all up front worshiping, giving, and receiving.

Worship is a contact sport. But then another time, the presence of the Lord felt like Papa God was in the room with us and He was playing with His kids. One teen came up and said he wanted to stage dive. I said, "Go for it." Suddenly, over a hundred people, including the speakers, started doing it. It was so fun. The feeling in the middle of worship was like Papa [was] playing with us—we were in His presence.

## Worship that brings you into the freedom to experience God as a child is quite a stretch for many.

We have put worship in a category of God up there and we're down here. Somehow trying to get our words out in worship to God, to be believable and plausible to Him in Heaven. It's the face to face with God—that's what allows us to show

Him, and each other, our joy and love. We're going to lay hands on people and bless them during worship. We want the "as it is in Heaven, so it is on earth" to be a reality in the midst of worship.

## What happens when you shift your thoughts so you are worshiping from Heaven to earth—rather than the way we usually do it—from our seat on earth staring up to Heaven?

There are no limits in worship. When I pastored in the Vineyard, I stretched the limits of Vineyard worship. People think we are over the edge but there are places in the Lord where we can go that we haven't gone before. There are still places to go. We haven't exhausted that yet, and never will.

In 1990 I went to Heaven and thought I was going to die. I saw sounds, heard colors, things that were happening in Heaven that I never experienced before. That was the beginning of [my] desire to do worship differently. I'd get up early and go out to a park and just play my guitar. I did that for years. I began to look at paths that had not been walked through yet. We wanted to enter into the place in worship we'd never been before. And now, we are starting to see that on occasion.

I had a bass player who was overcome with the anointing and God was all over him during this one particular worship time. One day, I turned around to see what was going on, because the skill level was beyond anything I had ever heard coming from him—and I saw the bass playing by itself. His eyes were wide open with shock and he later said he felt arms around him while he was playing, but his hands were not touching the strings.

On another occasion in my travels, a bass simply sitting on a stand during another meeting was also playing by itself.

During that time I had three different occasions where I went by the Spirit to other places on the earth and had conversations with a few people. Phenomenal things happen in the place of worship that take us out of the earthly realm into the heavenly realm.

Worship continues to evolve as people awaken to the fact that more of the anointing is available. In the coming days, we will discover that we have moved from a sound that enables individuals to connect with the heart of God, to a new sound that shifts the atmosphere of a church or a region and opens up Heaven more completely. The new sound will transform us. It will anoint us with fresh revelation of who Jesus really is and what He is up to in this generation. It will reveal the power that resides in the anointing.

Ray Hughes, the president and founder of Selah Ministries,4 has been in full-time ministry for 40 years. He received his Doctorate of Divinity in 1996 and is considered to be one of the foremost authorities on worship and its biblical foundations. He has given 25 years to extensive research into the biblical foundations of praise and the ways God uses the power of sound and praise to demonstrate His love and faithfulness to His people. This research has been developed into multiple teaching series for the purpose of training and releasing new generations of musicians, worship leaders, and worship teams.

When he spoke at Bethel Church in Redding, California, in August, 2010, he spoke about a new anointing emerging in the days to come—an anointing that shifts the atmosphere through worship.

"Exploring the science of sound can draw us into deeper revelations of God's nature and purposes. In the same way that there is a correlation between sound being released and a shift in the atmosphere, when praises are exuded from God's people, the environment changes and lives are impacted for eternity. God is raising up Davidic worshipers who will release a new sound, causing all creation to align with the Word of God and *'make a joyful noise'"* (see Ps. 66:1 KJV).

Ray, who is well educated in ethnomusicology, conducts a great deal of historical research. He recognizes certain correlations between musical notes and letters of the Hebrew alphabet. He gave an example of what happens when we intentionally release certain sounds of Heaven. When the Israelites struck the chords on their instruments that corresponded with the name of God according to the Hebrew alphabet, they were intentionally playing the name of, presence of, and nature of God. As a result, they released the power, presence, and purpose of God into the atmosphere.

They created an atmosphere of intention where people would shout the mighty acts of God into the next generation. Psalms emerged and were recorded that continue to break open the atmosphere and release revelation of the nature of God and His anointing of love and power.

Samuel also taught the band of prophets how to release the sound of Heaven. In one story, the company of prophets came down from a hill releasing their sound and, when they played, they released an anointing that transformed the nature of Saul as the revelatory anointing came upon him (see 1 Sam. 10). According to Ray, there is a power released in worship that releases the sounds of Heaven that dramatically transform a person or a place.

Ray asked the question:

Where are the musicians in this generation that are carrying something of the resonance of the power and presence of God so that when they play there is not just a soulish appeasement; but who will release the sound of Heaven into the atmosphere so that no one will be the same in that environment?

It is a good question. It is not an anointing we can work up. But according to Ray, there is hope for a whole new level of worship to emerge:

> There is a wind that carries the sound of Heaven that is going to carry us into the new thing of God—a sound that will release all the fullness of God's power into this generation.

Awakening to the anointing is something that does not just mark the beginning of knowing Jesus. We are coming into a Great Awakening and worship will release that wake-up call and transform the atmosphere so that Heaven comes to earth and no one will ever be the same. The awakened man, woman, or child will truly know the love of God in a deeply personal way and become a true worshiper who freely enters into the realms of Heaven and touches the heart of Jesus. New worship sounds will break open the atmosphere and the fullness of God will flood in like nothing this generation has ever seen before.

Clearly, God will always inhabit the praises of His people. But there is more to come as we face the winds of worship.

## Endnotes

1. For more information about Georgian Banov, go to: www.globalcelebration.com.

2. For more information about Carl Tuttle, go to: www.carltuttle.com.

3. For more information about Danny Steyne, go to: www.themountain.org.

4. For more information about Ray Hughes, go to: www.selahministries.com.

Chapter Three

# STEPPING INTO
# YOUR SACRED DESTINY

You, personally, have a sacred destiny and calling. How far into it do you want to go?

Have you awakened to Him? Does your heart burn when you feel His presence? Have you stood with your face to the wind of worship and caught a glimpse of the realities of Heaven surrounding you? There is more anointing to come. The oil is being released.

We all, corporately, have a sacred destiny and calling as well. Each generation is called to move into greater maturity in Christ, become established in Him, and release the revelation of Jesus. They release not only the stories of the great miracles of God in their generation and past moves documented in history, but also a very present anointing that reveals more about who Jesus really is—His character and personality—and the power that He manifests currently here on earth.

As each generation awakens to the Anointed One—we experience His love and presence and power, and we want more. We want to become established in Him. As we are established, we see ourselves becoming transformed more into His image and less into the image this fallen world would impose upon us. Our hearts long to experience more of His love filling us when we awaken to Him. Then we move into deeper relationship that establishes us in His love and we desire now to give it away, to impart it to others. What does imparting His love look like? Reaching out with compassion, we move in power to heal others emotionally, spiritually, physically. Moving out in power, we stop for the one God stops for, listening for the divine appointment that occurs as we take notice of another. The Holy Spirit drops a word of knowledge or wisdom or discernment into our spirit and we stop to impart that to the other, unlocking his or her heart and awakening it to the Anointed One.

As we learn to move in harmony with His Spirit, we find ourselves flowing into greater release. The gifts of the Spirit become integrated into our personalities and lifestyles. Some carry this anointing of His presence into their everyday work world and shift the atmosphere, releasing light in the darkness. Others release the anointing into governmental spheres of influence and transform policies and procedures in their companies and organizations that shift them out of the worldly system and into godly, spiritual principles that work.

Part of my destiny, and all of our destinies, is to release the anointing in everyday life—to our families, our colleagues, our bosses, our employees, to whatever chain of command or governmental structure we labor under. We are called to be like Christ and release His presence wherever we go. The rest of our destiny unfolds gradually, or suddenly, as a dream or vision imparts a revelation of destiny.

Apart from a dramatic God encounter releasing a word of destiny, coming into the awareness of your personal destiny seems to progress something like this: As you recognize who you are in Christ, and who

He is to you, you become established in Him. Your gifts, natural and spiritual, begin to converge and merge with your identity as a beloved son or daughter of the Creator of the universe. The favor of the Lord blows a breath of new life in you, quickening your faith and anointing, and ushers you into specific assignments or mandates.

As you begin to fulfill those assignments, suddenly, you realize that you are walking into your sacred destiny. Adventure and excitement renew your energy level. Suddenly, you are not old, but moving in the power of the Holy Spirit. Suddenly, you are not young and immature, but moving in wisdom and power beyond your training and years. Destiny unfolds and you begin to discover that every experience you have lived, every talent you possess, converges into a season of time. You find yourself empowered like never before to walk in your sacred destiny. You know who you are and where you are going. You know the purpose of the anointing in your life. You are walking in the anointing and it feels good.

## Becoming Established in the Anointing

Once we understand the route Jesus took to walk in His anointing, I believe we will get there more quickly. Jesus the man grew up and into the anointing, understood His sacred destiny, and began to walk toward that destiny. The Holy Spirit unleashed the two things He needed to survive life and fulfill His destiny—authority and power. Let's look at how Jesus became established in His anointing and sustained the anointing.

First, Jesus stepped into the awareness of His authority as established through the Word of God.

During His baptism the heavens opened. Jesus received the Father's affirmation and was filled with the Holy Spirit (see Luke 3:21-22). He understood that He carried the authority of His Father; but as a result of that public affirmation others came into the realization that

Jesus was someone special. They were waking up. They now knew that Jesus walked in a greater authority than John, but were soon to discover that His authority went beyond the ability to speak with wisdom and words that transformed lives. What enabled His authority to become manifest to others was this—Jesus became full of the Holy Spirit at baptism. Heaven was opened and the Holy Spirit descended on Him like a dove. In Luke 4:1-2 we see the importance of Jesus' encounter with the Holy Spirit emphasized.

> *Jesus, full of the Holy Spirit, returned from the Jordan and was led by the Spirit in the desert, where for forty days He was tempted by the devil....*

He needed the affirmation of the Father and the presence of the Holy Spirit to withstand the ordeal in the desert that became the ultimate test of His authority. The resulting tests caused Him to become stronger in His identity—to understand the power in speaking God's Word. In Jesus' weakness, after prolonged fasting, He realized the power of the Word. And the devil left Him..."*until an opportune time*" (Luke 4:13).

Something else transpired in the desert that remains hidden from us. Jesus went into the desert "...*full of the Holy Spirit*..." (Luke 4:1), but He came out in the power of the Holy Spirit (see Luke 4:14). Jesus shifted from acting solely through authority and shifted into evident **dunamis** power. And He knew what that power was for and stated it clearly.

> *...He has anointed me to preach good news to the poor. He has sent me to proclaim freedom for the prisoners and recovery of sight for the blind, to release the oppressed...* (Luke 4:18).

He went into the wilderness and stood against the enemy with the Word alone, knowing He carried the authority to rebuke the enemy. He came out full of the *power* of the Spirit, knowing that He had the power to overcome the works of the enemy. I believe that Jesus actually came out of the wilderness full of four specific types of power: *dunamis, exousia, ischuó,* and *kratos.*

The anointing became manifestly known as the convergence of these four different types of power. *Dunamis,* one of the Greek words for power, refers to God's ability to do mighty works, His miraculous power, might and strength flowing through Jesus and His disciples. It is used 120 times in the New Testament; more than any other Greek word for power. *Dunamis* was needed to triumph over the enemy and transfer the kingdom of this world to the dominion of the Kingdom of God.

*Exousia,* another Greek word for power, refers to the power to act, authority, as in delegated power. It refers to the authority God gives to His saints, authorizing them to act to the extent they are guided by faith (His revealed Word). Luke spoke about the combined power and authority that rocked their world:

> *Amazement came on all, and they spoke together, one with another, saying, "What is this word? For with authority and power He commands the unclean spirits, and they come out!"* (Luke 4:36 WEB).

Both authority and power are necessary to accomplish any task.

Jesus sustained both His authority and power by retreating from the crowds, and venturing off alone to spend time with the Father in prayer. Even Jesus had to tend His relationship with the Father. If He did, how much more do we need to spend time alone with the Father to sustain the authority and anointing in our lives? That alone time strengthened Him with two other types of power: *ischuó* and *kratos. Ischuó* means to be strong and have power. It refers to the Lord strengthening believers with combative, confrontational force to achieve all He gives faith for. That is, facing necessary resistance that brings what the Lord defines as success—His victory.

*for everyone born of God overcomes the world. This is the victory that has overcome the world, even our faith. Who is it that overcomes the world? Only he who believes that Jesus is the Son of God* (1 John 5:4-5).

*Kratos* refers to the might of God that strengthens us to endure morally, physically, mentally, and spiritually. Colossians 1:11 (WEB) brings us back full circle to understanding that we need all four types of power to endure and to overcome the world:

*strengthened with all power* [dunamis], *according to the might* [kratos] *of His glory, for all endurance and perseverance with joy...* (WEB).

Authority results solely from relationship with God. In Matthew 7:21-23, Jesus explains that not everyone will be welcomed into Heaven. They will say, "Hey, didn't we do this and that in Your name?"

And Jesus will reply, "Depart from Me! You took the power and used the gifts, but you never really wanted to know Me."

They moved in power but not authority. They failed to recognize that they were sons and daughters of the Lord, moving under His authority according to His will. As a result, the Lord will not endorse them. Using the power and the gifts was all about them—*"Look at me—whoopee!"* They failed to become established in their identities and know God on a more intimate level and honor the Anointed One above their anointing. As a result, they failed to step into true authority. When you walk in true Kingdom authority, your walk and your talk bear Heaven's seal of approval.

Becoming established in God involves the same process. We come to know how the Father sees us—not as sinners (Jesus took care of that), but as beloved daughters and sons in whom He is well pleased and whom He has predestined to inherit the Kingdom. We walk in His authority and as we study the Word, we begin to know how powerful that Word is—powerful to divide soul and spirit; to release revelation and conviction; to bless and to build up; or to destroy and condemn. We learn that our words are powerful. We grow in character that enables us to move and speak in love, graciously blessing and not cursing, knowing that as we move into our established places in the Kingdom of God, one day the words we speak will not fall to the ground. Our words will carry the weight and power that will create miracles—as we speak them. Authority is powerful. Not many have experienced the ability to speak and have it come to pass. But the potential is there.

The full weight of our authority is seen as we persevere through our testings in life and emerge filled with the power of the Holy Spirit. Anointing, then, becomes known not just as a divine enabling to fulfill a mission or a mandate, or to move a crowd into His presence through worship or prophetic revelation. Anointing becomes the convergence of authority (*exousia*) and power (*dunamis*) to transfer the kingdom of this world to the Kingdom of God.

## Carrying the Anointing

Once you are established in your authority—recognizing who you are in Christ and who He is to you—how do you carry the anointing and use it for a specific purpose? You start where you are, and you move on. You start by learning about and releasing the gifts that God gave you, and by learning to live and work in Him and through Him, imparting His gifts to others, for His glory. You learn how to carry the anointing as you go. And along the way, you realize that the anointing is not about you. You are empowered (*endunamou*) to fulfill His purpose on earth and enjoy the adventure of living in the Spirit. As you go, you discover that you can do all things through Christ who strengthens, or empowers (*endunamou*), you (see Phil. 4:13).

Bobby Conner, a former Baptist pastor who is world renowned for his prophetic anointing and international ministry, gives us the Lord's essential, urgent message to the Church about what it means to carry the anointing:

> ...The apostle Paul's deepest longing was not just to see his fellow believers, but to see them *in order to give them a gift.* As an apostle, his heart's motivation was not merely to teach, plant churches, work miracles or establish apostolic order— but to *give* all that he had to give, to *impart* what God has bestowed upon him, to lavish spiritual gifts generously upon *others,* that they "may be established."

> Imparting to the saints must be the heart's passion of all believers. The longing to impart is God's heart: He longs to pour Himself into His family, to equip believers to prepare them for relationship with Him as well as the work of service (see Ephesians 4:11-12). All grace and enabling comes only *from* Christ and *for* Christ, so we should delight in being an instrument to help others advance in their call, not ours. The Lord calls us to aide others first—not our own ministries first—to go higher in relationship with the Lord. We must never, never forget this fundamental tenet of the faith: freely we have received; freely we must *give* (see Matthew 10:8). Our goal is the establishing of the King in His kingdom, helping others discover their God given destiny and prepare them to better function in their high and heavenly calling (see Ephesians 1:18).

> This Greek word translated impart, *metadidómi,* is comprised of two smaller Greek words, *meta* and *didómi. Meta* means *with* as to walk *with* someone, an ally. *Didómi* is an extravagant word that means more than simply *giving.* The Greek suggests *profusion* and *abundance*—a complete "giving over" to another's care and trust. *Didómi* suggests, "to give forth

fully from oneself." To *impart*, then, or metadidómi, means to *give with profusion from the depths of oneself.* This "giving over" is the same word used to describe how the sea "gives over" that which is hidden beneath. From the depths of God Spirit, through our spirit, impartation comes forth.

As marvelous as this impartation sounds, there is a catch: we cannot *give* what we do not *have!* If we are to impart, we first must have something to release. To be able to impart, one first has to be *anointed* with the substance to impart. These two spiritual realities of impartation and anointing are different, but they relate and work together as the Spirit leads. How does this happen?

Here is a marvelous truth of the Kingdom of God: when we preach, teach, or minister in Love, in the Spirit of God, we impart the *substance* of Christ, not simply *information* about Him.

Jesus affirmed the prophetic promise of Isaiah 61:1-5:

*"The Spirit of the Lord is upon me, because He has anointed me to preach the gospel to the poor...."* (Luke 4:18).

For us to be anointed means that a divine enabling rests upon us. What is this enabling? This anointing is no less than Christ Himself: the Greek word translated *anoint* is the same word from which we derive the name Christ, *chrió!* What does it mean to have *chrió?* or to be anointed? It means to carry *the Christ*, the Anointed One! This same anointing consecrated our King for His Messianic office and gave Him the *power* to administer His Kingdom. This is the anointing we host—the Lord Jesus Christ resting upon us and in us, the Person of the Holy Spirit Himself. To be anointed is to be smeared and filled with Christ. In the Hebrew, *anoint* or *mashach*, means to *smear a liquid* or to *consecrate*. In other words, as believers in Christ Jesus, we are consecrated as holy priests to minister in His name, anointed by Him and *with Him*. He is the anointing!

Where does true anointing and power come from? The Spirit of God! We do not minister out of fine-tuned, educated human ability—but Holy Spirit anointing, that we then *impart*.

Here is the Lord's essential, urgent message to the Church: *we must learn to live and work in and through Him, the Anointed One—not by our own will and strength.*

*We must learn to impart Christ, the anointing—not our own ideas and agendas.*[1]

## Moving in Authority & Anointing

Out of authority, we can impart the presence and power of Christ to others at will. But learning to catch the wave of the anointing, and do what you see the Father doing, takes a degree of sensitivity to the Spirit and knowing the boundaries of your authority in that moment. No one articulates this better than Bill Johnson,[2] pastor of Bethel Church in Redding, California, and author of several books including *When Heaven Invades Earth*. His anointing as an apostle of faith, who increases faith in the goodness of our God who delights to heal and restore, is well known throughout the world. Bethel's School of Supernatural Ministry draws thousands of students from around the world every year as Bill Johnson's mandate leads him to impart an unprecedented anointing to this generation to move in supernatural power on the planet today.

During an interview with Bill in his office, he had this to say about the anointing:

I always equate the anointing with the person of the Holy Spirit and His presence. I don't separate it as a virtue or see it as something that is separate from Him, from the actual person. It seems to me that the anointing comes in flavors— like there's a certain characteristic or nature to that aspect of the presence. It says in Luke 5:17, *"The power of the Lord was present...to heal...."* Well, the power of God creates, the power of God destroys, the power of God does a lot of things, but there was an aspect of presence that was there specifically for healing. So it came in a flavor or a characteristic or an expression. The anointing seems to be the presence of the Lord that has, from God's view, a specific expression in mind. You know what it's like to have the anointing for writing come on you, and things just flow easily, or the anointing for revelation. Well, it's all the presence, but it comes with a certain characteristic or manifestation. When we move in the anointing, we're learning to recognize the presence first of all, and then secondly what He's there for.

When Jesus recognized in Luke 5 that the power of the Lord was present to heal, He knew that this was a healing moment. It wasn't a preaching moment; it wasn't a prophecy moment; it was a specific moment for healing and that presence comes with the heartbeat of Heaven. In His presence you can do a lot of different things. There's a slight sense that there's a certain anointing in the room and you can go into healing, or into prophecy, and you can go into a lot of things at any time, because of the presence there. But learning to recognize the unique manifestation of His presence is a big deal.

Say that the anointing is present for healing, and I only recognize the presence is there so I think it'd be a good idea to prophesy. I could still prophesy, but it will have a measured impact. But when I find what the Spirit of the Lord is present for, the sky's the limit. All the gifts are available at all times, so He's able to function in any one of these things, but learning to recognize what He's there for—that's when stuff blows up. That's when it's off the charts. We can move in healing any time in a meeting because of authority and we can draw from His presence. But when the power of the Lord is present to heal, it blows up, and that's the difference.

Luke 9:1 says, "...He gave [His disciples] power and authority...." Power has to do with the dunamis. It's catching the wave. It's sensing what the Lord is doing, paddling in the right direction, catching that wave, and moving with Him. So preached on Sunday night, and I sense the healing presence of Jesus come into the back, right section of the room. I stopped. I announced what I saw, and prostate cancer was instantly healed when the decree came.

The point is, we operate in authority. The power came in during the meeting; I shifted; and I stopped the direction of the meeting. That is what I mean mean by paddling to catch a wave. As soon as I caught the wave, I announced what happened. When that happened, cancer was healed. A woman with a tumor in her breast was healed. As a friend touched her shoulder, the thing dissolved; it disappeared on the spot. It happened because power came into the room.

Power is catching a wave. Authority is starting a wave. Authority is operating out of who He says you are to get a breakthrough. And the anointing is the wave.

The Word says Jesus only did what He saw His Father do, so people will say, "Now wait a minute, that's catching the wave. How can you start a wave and say you only do, or He only did what He saw His Father do?"

You understand the conflict of concepts. But the issue is this: our authority is written into the sovereignty of God. So sometimes I can only discover what the Father is doing by using my authority. That means it does not all come to me directly. Jesus only did what He saw His Father do, so what about the woman who touched His clothing? (See Matthew 9.) That wasn't deliberate on His end. He turned and saw what the Father was doing because He recognized that presence, that faith on her.

In the situation of the Syro-Phoenician woman who wanted her daughter delivered in Mark 7, Jesus in essence said, "Healing is not for your people." Jesus recognized in her response the work of the Father and released the miracle. So the point is, it doesn't always come directly; sometimes it's discovered by use of authority.

When you're down at the mall and you're going to pray for somebody, there's no worship team, there's nobody setting an atmosphere where there's power moving through the mall—it's all authority. That's how we can get what happens in the four walls of the church out of the four walls of the church. It's through authority. And then what happens is in the authority position, something starts breaking loose. Suddenly you've got both working—authority and anointing. You've got like what happened for Chad Dedmond years ago down at the grocery store where a deaf woman and somebody with carpal tunnel syndrome were healed, and God gave someone else a hip replacement. Suddenly, there was power moving through the grocery store and both caught a wave and started one. It is an interesting dynamic to see the two work together, but both are needed.

You always operate out of who you are and what God has assigned you to do. Whatever our status, God gives each one of us a taste of where we are not yet, in order to draw us into something more. Why? Because He wants us to know there is more. We have to remain childlike to get there. He'll let us taste of something that's beyond our norm.

That's what a gift of faith does. A gift of faith absolutely works every time. It's for a specific incident or situation. So when the gift of faith comes, I taste of a measure of faith I don't know as a lifestyle. So here's my lifestyle of faith and anointing that's been building for all these years. I've reached a certain level, but then I taste a higher level. I don't immediately move up to this level, but I move toward it. The draw is there. I'm not where I was, but neither am I at the place I just tasted.

So whether you're affecting a neighborhood, your family, a city, or a nation, there's always more. You have to remain childlike to get into the next level of anointing. Every new level is entered as a child; it's not entered as an expert.

You know, it's natural to hunger for the impossible. Everybody does. If they don't, it's only because they have bad teaching, or they've been disappointed. Those two things will kill the hunger, but it's in you. It's the DNA of Christ. We're born again; we carry His DNA. It isn't normal not to hunger for it. The best way to deal with bad teaching or disappointment is to start creating hope by modeling an experience you don't yet have.

All of us have the authority to impart the Anointing, who is Christ, and release the gifts of the Spirit according to the need of the person who stands before us. Not many of us have the opportunity to consistently stand before a crowd and move in the anointing, under the empowerment of the Holy Spirit. Those who do realize that at some point, they had to stop moving in their own agendas and learn how to flow with the Holy Spirit to accomplish His desire. They had to learn how to recognize the wave of His Spirit, paddle out and catch it, then ride it in. There are longboard surfers like me who like to ride the smaller waves that break for a long ride sideways toward the shore. And there are big-wave surfers who are towed behind Jet Skis® to catch giant waves —waves of enormous power that can crush them if they fall.

Most of my peers, who were once on fire and serving the Lord in various positions of ministry, have left all ministry involvement and settled into the easy chairs of middle age or focused on their own recreational pursuits. They will peek in on the waves of renewal or outpouring once in awhile, but really want nothing to do with this current move of God. They have been there and done that. Sadly, many pastors, prophets, apostles, evangelists, and teachers, who used to watch for the waves and ride them with ease, have also stopped paddling out to meet the waves.

As a former surfer, I can tell you this timeless truth—the waves never stop coming. Big waves come in sets. Every season stirs up the waters and beckons surfers to enter in. Stormy seas generate the biggest, most awesome waves. The waves are still calling us. It's time for some to get off the beach, break out the board, and paddle out.

Sometimes, however, we need to recognize that transition God calls us into—out of the lineup and into instructor/mentor mode. We carry different anointings and authority during different seasons of our lives. Big-wave surfers must turn the lineup over to younger surfers eventually—for a reason. The spirit is willing, but age and wisdom take over and wisely invite them to step into another manifestation of the anointing they are able to carry and sustain in that season of life. We are seeing this transition coming quickly in the Church today. More big waves are coming, and many in leadership today are training the next generation to catch them.

If you have awakened to His love and power, you have a destiny that can only be fulfilled by you. You have a place and position in the corporate, mystical Body of Christ on earth and you have a sacred calling. Time is short. I suggest you get on with discovering who you really are and who you are destined to become. God is not finished with you yet. All of your gifts, experiences, and anointings have converged at this stage of your life for a purpose. God is calling you to become someone more than you ever dreamed. He has need of you to step into the authority and anointing He has destined for you to release at this stage of your life. Will you come into the next level of your anointing?

## Endnotes

1. Bobby Conner, "Anointing and Impartation: Ministering His Substance, Part 1," March 19, 2010, www.bobbyconner.org/Articles.cfm?id=61. Used with permission from EaglesView Ministries.

2. For more information about Bill Johnson, go to: www.bjm.org.

# SECTION II

# SHIFTING SHADOWS
# OF DECEPTION

**Julia:**

So, who are the ones You are calling to carry the anointing of Your love and Your power; how will we recognize them as they emerge in the days to come?

**Jesus:**

*They are examples of My mercy; extensions of My grace. One who has been forgiven much, loves much, and walks in a new dimension of faith, hope, and love. Because they walk, live, and dwell so close to My heart, they are able to impart that to others. There is no judgmentalism in them. They judge not because they know that My love suspends judgment, and they feel the embrace of My total acceptance...an acceptance they could never earn...a love that will never be denied or withheld.*

*Their humility is the conduit of power.*

*Their ability to honor others and move within a team mentality increases their authority and provides the safety I desire for them.*

*They are not afraid to share their testimonies because they are not ashamed of the Gospel of Christ; for they know it is the power of God unto salvation. And the very anointing that breaks the hold of the enemy on cultures is this power of God unto salvation—released through the word of their testimony and the ever-increasing revelation of My blood.*

*They are not a remnant cowering in caves. They are leaders taking lands, tribes, and nations. They are filled with a holy boldness that comes from being My favored one, My beloved, called by My name, born to inherit nations, born specifically in this hour of history, for this hour.*

*They are the new liberation theology I am turning loose on the world. Sent as reminders of grace and mercy, they have laid down weapons of carnal warfare and traded them in for a revelation of extreme love.*

*And they will know My love in the days to come. Each one, personally...shockingly...stunned beyond reason, stupefied and abandoned to all but Me. Just one touch of My love transforms the most broken and orphaned into a holy, anointed child in whom is all My delight. And they will come...en masse.*

*They will be the forerunners of a love revolution I am sending to wash the earth like a flood as in the days of Noah; a flood not to destroy, but to heal the land.*

*Because they bear the marks of Christ on their bodies, the scars etched across their souls, the emblems of suffering evident in their emotional scars and skin markings, some will embrace them. Others will shun them.*

*And to the ones who cannot receive them, tell them this: "Go and learn what this means: 'I desire mercy, not sacrifice. For I have not come to call the righteous, but sinners" (Matt. 9:13).*

Chapter Four

# ABORTING THE ANOINTING

There comes a sacred moment in the life span of a pregnancy called "the quickening." Right about the end of the fourth month, as the woman begins to show the obvious signs of pregnancy, she suddenly feels the first fluttering kicks of the infant inside of her. There is no denying it. She is carrying something, someone, some creative life force with her, and it is only a matter of time before it will be released.

That is the sacred moment of awe when everything that is unseen becomes real, and the vision of what is unseen will soon become manifest. It is the time when a woman grows excited and feels most alive and thrilled to know that all is OK, and joy fills her like never before. It is also a time of fears for what will be. Emotions flood in with a rush of hormones like never before. She feels like a crazy artist who cannot contain herself because she is pregnant with possibility, with vision, with new life that longs for expression. What she is feeling is a "quickening anointing"—a moment when faith leaps up and says, "This is happening…a new life is about to become."

It is that way with the anointing, too.

During the first months when God impregnates you with vision, it is so easy to lose that vision, or dream, or desire. Until the time of quickening, it seems like you are walking only by faith and a hazy intuition that something is being formed within you. It's easy to abort the anointing because you cannot grasp what it will look like when it has fully materialized. It is easy to speak it away because you are wondering, "Has God really said this?" "Has God really released His dream, His vision, His idea within me?" "Will He bring it to pass?"

Or you can walk away too quickly as your thoughts of shame and pain cause you to feel unworthy to carry the beauty of God within you. And you say, "I am not good enough to carry this vision. I am too damaged to be seen. If you only knew where I have been and what I have been doing, you would not fault me for aborting this vision. I have other plans for my life and I cannot carry this dream, this idea, this mission to full term, much less parent it into viability."

Many people seem to abort God's destiny and purpose in their lives almost as soon as they realize God has a sacred destiny and purpose for them. And as I reach back into my memory, I know that my pain was not only what drove me to Jesus; it was also the the subconscious motivator for all my efforts to sabotage the anointing of God in my life. Although I knew God's love, I could not run with joy in what God had given to me. I was hindered by pain, shame, grief, loss, and guilt. I was also afraid of the revelation and power that I experienced.

While living in Israel, immediately after receiving the baptism of the Holy Spirit, the heavens were open to me. I began seeing angels and demons, having accurate words of knowledge about people I met on the street, and trusting my prophetic intuition that kept me out of harm's way while traveling in a country under constant threat of terrorist activity and religious persecution. I had no prior experience of Christianity so I thought that this heightened spiritual sensitivity was the normal Christian life.

Eventually, as I moved back to the U.S., I thought I was a freak. No other Christians I met had that level of seeing and experiencing the spiritual realm. So I kept quiet and tried desperately to quench the Spirit. After all, I had a degree to finish at a secular university.

I was able to shut most of the revelation down, but not all. When the prophetic movement popularized in Kansas City by Mike Bickle merged with the healing movement of the Vineyard, I suddenly felt "saved." I could come out of hiding because I finally learned that countless others around the world believed what I believed about the normal Christian life. They agreed that it includes the ability to walk in the spiritual realm of Heaven while here on Earth. Like me, they believed in the Christian's ability to do and see and hear the same things Jesus did. I wanted to grow in my understanding and in the gifts. I was excited, but felt unworthy. That sense of unworthiness stemmed from past sins and wounds that I, for some reason, thought disqualified me from carrying the anointing. Added to that was the fact that I am a woman and women's gifts are not often received in many churches.

I have been on the verge of spontaneously aborting or sabotaging His purpose and destiny several times in my life. Each time, God decided to give me a strong revelation of Himself in order to help me move on. He gave me three open visions that revealed to me exactly what I needed to prevent me from aborting the anointing—each one was a revelation of the cross.

My life is a life of knowing that God has pursued me. And I know one thing—the revelations of the cross and the blood are central to persevering in faith and receiving the quickening anointing that activates my faith over and over again.

## Come Down From the Cross of Your Own Making

Once, several years ago, I had finished speaking during one of the sessions of a Santa Barbara business conference and decided to forgo lunch to visit the old mission. Hummingbirds buzzed through the warm spring air of the mission garden as I walked up the path. The scent of earth and stone baking in the sun led me to take shelter from the rays. I moved inside the cool chapel just as a few tourists wandered out, leaving me alone.

I sat awhile in the front pew of the small chapel and stared at the almost life-sized wooden statue of Christ on the cross, a grisly sight. Suddenly, the room blurred and I found myself catapulted out of my seat and onto the cross. Sobbing, I felt the pain of the nails in my hands and feet. I moved my head to see the rivers of blood pouring out of me. Just as suddenly, I caught sight of a man leaping off the pew, moving rapidly toward me me. He brought His shoulder beneath mine to catch my fall then reached up to pull the nails from my hands. I slumped over His shoulder, and He reached down to pull the spike from my feet. It was the Lord.

He sobbed loudly, in agony over my agony. "I never meant for you to be there," He sobbed. "I never meant for you to take My place."

The vision lasted a few seconds. As abruptly as it came, it faded. And I found myself still seated on the pew, tears streaming down my face.

You cannot purchase life or atone for your own sins. Why memorialize the pain by crucifying yourself over the sins others have committed against you? Why allow the memories to nail you to the cross of despair? Life and forgiveness are freely given to you. Long before you were born, He chose you, called you by name, and said, "You are Mine. Will I not freely give you all things?"

The enemy loves to take a spiritual truth and twist it into something obscene. The cross of Christ is His alone. The cross He calls us to take up is not our suffering over old pain. His cross purchased your salvation. Your cross seeks to abort it.

Your cross perpetuates hopelessness, thinking that nothing will ever change.

His bloodshed ensures your healing.

Your cross and emotional bloodletting keeps your mind focused on carnal reasoning and glorifies the power of the enemy in your life.

His cross released power over death.

Your cross keeps you in a cycle of death.

His cross released grace to become fully alive, free from all that weighs you down—your sins and the sins that others have done against you.

Your cross prevents you from living life fully and walking into the destiny and purposes for which you were created. Even though you might feel dead, God, who is rich in mercy and full of kindness, is calling you into a place of resurrection.

*But because of His great love for us, God, who is rich in mercy, made us alive with Christ even when we were dead in transgressions—it is by grace you have been saved. And God raised us up with Christ and seated us with Him in the heavenly realms in Christ Jesus, in order that in the coming ages He might show the incomparable riches of His grace, expressed in His kindness to us in Christ Jesus. For it is by grace you have been saved, through faith—and this not from yourselves, it is the gift of God—not by works, so that no one can boast. For we are God's workmanship, created in Christ Jesus to do good works, which God prepared in advance for us to do* (Ephesians 2:4-10).

You must choose to come off the cross of your own making. Only then can you take up the cross that God gives you. You are God's workmanship, created to do good works, not out of duty but out of a love that compels you to do what you were created to do in work, in relationships, and in ministry. His resurrection enabled you to be seated with Him in heavenly realms, a place where you can bear the pain of earthly suffering because, like Christ, you have already over-come and are already victorious. It is a mystery, I know. But more will be revealed as you choose life and ask God to lift you up into a higher perspective, from a viewpoint that transcends your earthly reasoning.

The cross God gives you is not one of suffering outrageously in the work He calls you to do or in the relationships impacting your life. It is a cross of the joy of intimately walking with Him and shar-ing in His sufferings for the purpose of transferring the dominion of darkness—satan's domain—into the Kingdom of light, Jesus' domain purchased so many years ago.

His death and resurrection call you to come up higher, to expe-rience the Kingdom power of God. The same resurrection power that raised Christ from the dead resides in you. Despair, depression and anxiety, pain and shame, and a sense of unworthiness may have worked some profit in your life in years past. But you don't need it any-more. Consider it part of your loss and let it go for the sake of Christ.

*But whatever was to my profit I now consider loss for the sake of Christ. What is more, I consider everything a loss compared to the surpassing greatness of knowing Christ Jesus my Lord, for whose sake I have lost all things. I consider them rubbish, that I may gain Christ and be found in Him, not having a righteousness of my own that comes from the law, but that which is through faith in Christ—the righteousness that comes from God and is by faith. I want to know Christ and the power of His resurrection and the fellowship of sharing in His sufferings, becoming like Him in His death, and so, somehow, to attain to the resurrection from the dead* (Philippians 3:7-11).

Where is this power of resurrection to be found? How do you access it? Many people believe that God can just reach out and touch them in their living rooms, bringing instant breakthrough. He can. Sometimes He does. But perhaps He has another plan. Perhaps He created His Body, the Church, to assist the work. So, not realizing that God's power resides in His Body, some people stay home, practice their defeatist attitudes, and passively pray something like, "Anytime, God. Come and get me."

Meanwhile, in a home group nearby or a church meeting within an hour's drive from home, God's presence and power routinely flood the meetings, releasing the fullness of salvation—forgiveness of sins and healing of disease, deliverance from oppression and release of gifts and purpose and destiny. Why stay home? I don't know about you, but I know where I'm going when I need something from God. I am going to travel to a place where my desperation meets God, who dwells wherever two or more are gathered in His name, and invite His Spirit to come and minister in a way that I cannot access on my own, alone, at home. I run to Him because I know this:

*Therefore, since we have a great high priest who has gone through the heavens, Jesus the Son of God, let us hold firmly to the faith we profess. For we do not have a high priest who is unable to sympathize with our weaknesses, but we have one who has been tempted in every way, just as we are—yet was without sin. (Hebrews 4:14-15).*

When I run to His throne of grace, He always meets me. He has never failed to back up His promise, "Draw near to Me and I will draw near to you" (see James 4:8). Where is this throne of grace? It is wherever you meet with God.

The Anointed One knows that you need more of His anointing of love and power—especially if you have been ministering your heart out, or laying down your life for your family or church or mission. He is calling some people to come down off the cross of their self-imposed martyrdom and give it up. He never meant for you to take His place.

The vision I had of the cross enabled me to shed the sense of unworthiness I felt and to embrace my destiny.

A revelation of the cross and the blood of Christ is different from being taught about it and taking communion as a remembrance of the mystery of union with Christ. Revelation personalizes everything. Suddenly, we know that Jesus didn't mean for us to be on the cross. And we understand that His blood makes us worthy. His righteousness is imparted to us through His sacrifice—not through our working to earn His forgiveness or striving to earn His love.

## Getting Naked Before God

The second vision I had of Jesus happened years later. For several months God's presence dwelt with me. It started with an encounter where the love of God annihilated me with a sudden bomb of love that unleashed over me like a waterfall. The full weight of rushing water flowed down from Heaven, crushed me, tumbled me, and humbled me as I felt His overwhelming love. His loving presence then moved in with me for about seven months. This season of visitation ended with a direct encounter with Jesus.

I was 30 years old and writing my first book; I had the contract in hand. Every morning, God spoke clearly to me, sometimes pulling the weeds from the garden of my heart, at other times bringing revelation and words of knowledge about others to me. Every night I dreamed accurate prophetic dreams. Angels seemed close at hand, and once during that time, I saw one stationed by my bed, watching over me. During that season, when I went to church and prayed during corporate intercession, everyone seemed captivated by the words flowing from my lips. I had spent so much time in His presence in prayer at home that I came armed with something to pray in public. I waited until I saw the big bubble of what I called the "spirit of prayer" come upon me, felt the stirring of anointing to stand up and pray, and people took notice of what they heard because the presence of God filled the room. I realized later that I was learning how to seek God's will, wait for the anointing, and then release what God had given me. It was the normal Christian life extended to others—not just in words, but in words that came forth carrying the power of God into the atmosphere to accomplish His will.

After a few months of visitation that left me feeling progressively holy and pure, I felt like Jesus was coming very, very close. Finally, He revealed Himself to me in person. It marked the dramatic end to that season of visitation. He came, and He went, and He didn't even speak!

He just walked past me on a Sunday morning in my home church, the Anaheim Vineyard Christian Fellowship, at the end of a conference where a prophet named Paul Cain had been speaking that week. The revelatory atmosphere was still electric. At times that week, I saw the veil parted between the natural and the spiritual realms. I saw angels moving about the room, and cartoon-like overlays on peoples' bodies revealing both emotional and physical sicknesses. I even heard the thoughts of others. I saw the angel that pointed out certain people to Paul before Paul would get up to speak. This was a whole other level of revelation. Rather than seeing one thing about one person at a time, I was seeing and hearing what was going on in the whole room of hundreds of people all at once. I was overwhelmed but excited. I could not imagine living in that constant state of "seeing."

I became frightened and was unsure how to respond to God now. There was no way I wanted to live with that burden of being constantly aware of what was going on with others around me. Because of my own fear, I was in danger of aborting the anointing and the calling on my life once again. I also knew that I was not a holy person. I had a sense that my lack of purity and holiness and my dysfunctional family upbringing, would undermine the gifts and the call on my life in the future. In order for me to survive the anointing in the years to come, God decided to release the revelation of His blood to me personally.

The room fell silent. Somewhat bored and tired, I stood singing the last song at the close of the service. Suddenly, every molecule in my body felt as if it were exploding outwardly—an instant annihilation! All the people in the church suddenly vanished. Then I saw Jesus stroll by the edge of the platform with a silly grin on His face. A slight breeze raised goose bumps on my skin and I felt naked. Horrified at the thought, I looked down at my body and yes—I was naked! Even worse, every sin I had ever committed—past, present, and future— was tattooed in fine script across every millimeter of my skin. As I literally contemplated my navel, I caught a glimpse of Jesus swiftly removing a simple robe from His shoulders and casually, with perfect aim, tossing it so that it wrapped itself around my shoulders. The weight of it plopped me back into my seat, and I came back to reality, bent over, crying with relief.

As for the robe, I came to understand that Jesus tossed the robe of righteousness over me to cover my sin so completely that neither I, nor others, could see or sense sin in me. God provided His righteousness as a covering for me. I am no longer prey for the enemy or his accusing thoughts, because I know that I know that my sins are forever covered.

We need a strong encounter with the Anointed One to reveal just what He accomplished on the cross and through His shed blood—a total repositioning of us into the place of right standing with Him.

Scripture equates righteousness with joy. Romans 14:17 says that the Kingdom of God is *"...a matter of righteousness, peace and joy in the Holy Spirit."* When you are rightly related to Jesus and His blood covers your sins, peace and joy will fill your heart. Shame and despair have no place in you. That robe of righteousness covers your thoughts and keeps you from temptation and self-annihilating attitudes. Imagine yourself wrapped in the robe of righteousness. Job said, *"I put on righteousness as my clothing..."* (Job 29:14). Ephesians encourages us *"to be made new in the attitude of your minds; and to put on the new self, created to be like God in true righteousness and holiness"* (Eph. 4:23-24).

The robe of righteousness will guard your thoughts and your ways. It will also guard your heart and mind when the enemy comes against you. If you are to move in the anointing of love and power, and to survive the anointing of ministry, you need to understand this in a deeply personal way.

Despite those strong visions of Jesus, I was unable to sustain the anointing. I burned out after a decade of intense ministry. Working with an inner-city church full of AIDS patients, confused homosexuals, mentally ill people, and university students took its toll on me. I ministered prophetically in the city and was well known for the revelatory gifts that flowed accurately and powerfully, releasing physical and emotional healing and calling forth destinies. This changed the hopelessness I saw in people into fresh faith for the future.

Along with the invitations to speak and minister came the enemy's backlash to demolish me, usually through the words of other Christian leaders. A secondary leader in a church, usually a pastor's wife or an elder, would invite me to speak at a meeting. I would minister my heart out, releasing very accurate prophetic words that brought healing to some, restored marriages, and quickened the destiny in others. Afterwards, the main pastor would inevitably comment, not on the ministry or what I said, but on the fact that I was a single woman. He would then say that he hadn't invited me and didn't appreciate having a single woman ministering in his church. I've heard things like, "Maybe next time you can return with your husband," implying that I should not be ministering unless it is in a secondary role. Pastors of this persuasion expected me to marry and play a supportive role that would make my future husband's ministry shine.

Even in my own church that I was helping to plant in an inner city, the pastor was prone to inviting young homosexual men to speak and shutting down any women who had any anointing. Once, after years of serving in the church and becoming known for the prophetic anointing I carried, he invited me to speak on a Sunday night and set the date. A couple of weeks prior to that date I called to confirm it with him. He replied that he had just been kidding. In fact, he had scheduled another young man in that evening service. That young man was someone who was struggling to come out of the homosexual lifestyle. His unspoken message to me and other women was this: "I would rather have a homosexual male speak in my church than a woman."

Over the years, I had more opportunities and invitations to speak in other churches around the world—but never in my home church. He also elevated married couples who joined the church above the single adults who displayed more anointing and wisdom, loyalty and character.

Clearly, the gender and marriage bias in the church wore me down with disappointment and hurt. Women received me as a prophet. Men didn't receive me at all—or they received me as a writer or a counselor, something supportive, someone they didn't feel like they had to compete against spiritually.

I found myself isolating, slipping into old sinful thoughts and behaviors and wanting out. While ministering to people in the church, I also worked full-time as a counselor (having just finished my Master's degree) and taught a couple of classes at a local college. Clearly, I was giving out too much and taking in too little. I had come to the point it felt like God was "using" me. The lack of personal support and anti-women sentiment in the church completely twisted my thoughts until I was walking in a state of mental deception. I began to feel like I had wasted my life on Jesus and He had given me nothing in return…not even the husband and a family that I had so long desired. I decided that my obsessional love for Jesus had ruined my life, and it was time to let it go.

I needed a vacation. So I took one. But I forgot to come back. I left the church and moved back to Southern California where walking the beach and being on, in, or under the water seemed to bring more healing to me than any anointed worship service ever could.

Years later, I found myself drowing—literally—one day while scuba diving in Hawaii. Slipping into unconsciousness, my eyes fought like children resisting bedtime, blinking back darkness, focusing on the light before me that was shrinking in on itself. I could not rouse myself, only surrender, let go. No noise but the deep and rhythmic breathing of a detached body that I knew was mine sounded in my ears. I could hear my life slowing down—no demands, no worries, no fear, no past or future, just a totally emotionless existence leading to oblivion. My face drifted lower, settling onto the ocean floor. I smiled. This was the way it should be: I was dropping nonchalantly from one life into the next.

"Get moving." I heard a voice closer to me than my own heartbeat, authoritative but gentle. My brain heard it and ignored it, until I felt two hands grab the straps of my buoyancy vest, pull me off the sand, flip me backward, and hurtle me toward the other divers. My feet reflexively kicked twice—my body squirming back into reality.

The action woke me reluctantly. Although slightly groggy, reason prevailed now. I finished the dive, swimming in the company of others, rose to the surface a few minutes early, and climbed over the transom of the dive boat, saying nothing on the return to Honokohau Harbor in Kona.

Had I completely passed out underwater, the others would not have noticed in time to rescue me. My jaw would have gone slack, the regulator fallen out of my mouth, and instead of sucking in air, I would have breathed water, convulsed, and died within minutes.

Angels swim. I know that now. Why one swam after me, pulled me away from the "pearly gates," and hurtled me back toward life was a mystery I pondered for many days afterwards. You cannot come that close to death without wondering why you were left to live.

"Why did You save me?" I questioned God out loud one day as I stared at the ocean and lay far off the balcony of the little Kona coffee shack I had rented for the month.

Three months later, God decided it was time to answer my question. By then, my heart had softened toward the Lord and I had made an arrangement with Him to amend the calling on my life. I would write about others and help build His Kingdom as a writer, so long as He enabled me to keep a lid on the revelatory gifts. That way, like a silly child, I thought I could control just when and where I would serve the Lord.

I had just started to write for Christian publications again and so I went to Seattle to write an article about Randy Clark's healing school, the first of many he still conducts around the world. I was walking into a setup.

During the very first evening worship set, I felt the presence of the Lord descend on me. The sheer weight of His presence caused my shoulders to slump forward. I felt myself involuntarily edging off the seat toward the floor until I was bowing low. I knew that I was encountering a rare, holy moment; it was an encounter with God Himself. I felt myself disintegrating in His presence, every molecule blowing apart. The church; the musicians a few yards away; the crowd standing, sitting, and dancing in the pews behind me and around me—all disappeared. All went silent.

Just then, the rumbling voice of the Lord spoke clearly to my mind, "This is why I saved you from the bottom of the sea."

I became aware of something hovering near to the right hemisphere of my brain, like a big bubble undulating just off to the side. The Lord spoke again, "I want to restore the anointing."

I realized that He was asking permission to release more of His Holy Spirit, His presence, and particularly, the revelatory gifts into my life.

When I said, "Yes," the weight lifted off and His presence broke into my entire being. Suddenly, I saw a movie-screen, close-up image of Jesus' face on the cross: the crown of thorns on His head, blood running down His face and patchy beard. The crown of thorns spoke of mockery as His tormentors abused a seemingly powerless Christ.

The gruesome image faded and I became aware of a man sitting next to me.

He took the crown of thorns off His head and held it out to me. The long spikes were familiar to me. I had seen these thorns while living in Israel many years ago. I felt them draw blood along my legs, gashing through my jeans as I rode horseback near the Sea of Galilee.

I drew back, hesitant for a scant second, and then reached out to take the crown of thorns in my hands, knowing that I would have to accept it, and place it on my head. Was this the anointing? A crown of mockery? Had I not mocked myself and endured the harsh words of others long enough to burn out and sail away from ministry, church, or anything religious for several years? But how can you refuse the Lord—especially when He is sitting right beside you?

Just as my fingers barely touched the crown of thorns, it transformed into a thin band of gold. The Lord watched my expression change from dread to delight as I took hold of the crown of gold. He smiled and said, "You wear the gold. I'll wear the thorns."

Then He faded away.

I was so overcome by emotion that I left the main room and crawled into the hospitality room where I lay on the floor and cried for almost an hour before my friends came looking for me and prayed for me. Then, as if God and I had shared a private joke, I broke into laughter for awhile before I could compose myself and walk back into the main meeting room where the speaker was just beginning his message.

The laughter and the tears had released all the residual emotions associated with the thorns in my past. As I walked back into the room, I felt joy and the courage to pick up, not my crown of thorns, but my crown of gold—the crown of beauty, life, glory, and honor; the crown of my calling, my future, my destiny reinstated with His spiritual authority and strength to persevere.

I had given up on God's plans for my life, tossed aside my crown of life (the royal crown that belongs to a child of God), and opted for a long vacation. But God had not given up on me. He knew the words that others had spoken against me through the years, mocking me for following Christ, criticizing me for the ways I ministered, speaking against me unjustly, denigrating the gifts because they came through the hands of a woman. He knew the words that settled onto my mind like a constricting crown of thorns.

He also knew the words that I spoke against myself, the silent negative tapes that cycled through my mind like a crown of thorns pricking me and drawing blood. He knew that all these words goaded me like thorns until I had had enough and decided to toss that crown of thorns aside. He let me take my time and rest from burnout so I could recover from the wounds of ministry, work, and life, for awhile. And just as I regained my joy and was having fun hanging out in octopuses' gardens in the shade, God decided our time would begin again.

He is the God of second chances. He is the second wind that suddenly fills our sails and moves us quickly across the oceans and deserts of our despair. When we cast down our crowns, or lose them by the wayside, He picks them up, holds onto them, and waits. He waits until we are ready to take hold of the crowns that we think are made of thorns. He does this knowing all along that He will wear the thorns and bear the brunt of our pain, while we wear the gold.

That third vision of Jesus quickened my faith to such a degree that all fear of the anointing and the fellowship of His sufferings, and potential burnout, fled. I was ready for anything and for nothing. For suddenly, I knew that I was no longer alone: Jesus would be by my side, and I was never to lose the awareness of His presence when I stepped out to go to work or to minister in a church or at a retreat. The quickening of my faith shattered the shame I had come to feel because of my singleness and my gender. I realized that He is "my Husband" and He will back up His Bride's written and spoken word.

Eventually, I came into an awareness that I was truly walking in a restored anointing and authority as a result of that vision. More importantly, the vision healed me to the point that it no longer mattered to me how people received me. It made no difference to me, even if they chose not to receive my gifts at all.

Regardless of gender, everyone, at some point in ministry and life, weakens and grows *"weary in well doing"* (Gal. 6:9 KJV). Perhaps you are in that place right now. Or perhaps, you have already aborted your anointing. God has not turned away from you. He is waiting patiently, lovingly, for you.

## The Crown and the Quickening

When you feel as if old guilt, shame, and pain overwhelm you, you need to ask for a revelation of the cross and the blood of Christ. When you feel like you have wandered away and aborted the plans and purposes of God in your life, you need to come back and ask for a quickening of your faith to see His grace and faithfulness covering your sins—past, present, and future. And then you need to take up your crown, to step back into your royal identity, and move on saying, "Quicken my faith with Your anointing, Lord, and I will go out and be Your anointed one, carrying Your presence and power into my every day. Here I am, draw me to You again and again, and then send me out, again and again."

As a writer, whenever I write a book a reader says, "I am so glad you wrote that…," what I am hearing is this: "I am so glad that you did not abort the vision that God gave you, the prophetic word that God wanted to release to me through you, the ministry I received."

As a speaker, or sculptor, or poet, or painter, or musician, when someone comes with tears in his or her eyes and nods at you, what that person is saying is this: "I am so glad that you brought that into the world…that you didn't abort your gift and your vision. I needed that. It connected me to God in a way that church never could."

Or they are saying, "The instrumental chords that you played lifted me into a vision of Heaven; your sermon changed my life; the touch of your loving hand released healing to my body, soul, and spirit; your prophetic words transformed the way I thought about myself and about God."

Don't abort the anointing that God quickens within you. Let your children come forth and say, "I am so glad that you didn't abort me."

Take up the crown of gold and you will feel the quickening anointing that you need. It will let you know who you are to Him. It will let you feel worthy enough to carry Him every day into your sphere of influence—to your friends, coworkers, family, community, workplace, church—and even to the end of the world.

Seek Him for the quickening anointing no matter what age you are. Suddenly, you will feel those first fluttering kicks of life stirring within you, and you will receive the impartation of faith to run with joy.

## The Quickening Anointing

The quickening anointing is the anointing to see the unseen that you are carrying and become empowered with the Holy Spirit who releases the excitement needed to persevere. It is the sudden inrush anointing of faith that enables you to persevere with joy! It is the sudden realization that what you hope for will actually happen, and what God has commanded into existence is His creation. What we are carrying did not come from anything that we had seen or created in and of ourselves; it is the Lord who is forming something within, and He will be faithful to bring it to birth. The quickening anointing releases a confidence and an assurance of faith that only comes from direct encounter with Him—either subtly or dramatically. Hebrews 11:1-3 speaks about this quickening of faith:

> *Faith is the confidence that what we hope for will actually happen; it gives us assurance about things we cannot see. Through their faith, the people in days of old earned a good reputation. By faith we understand that the entire universe was formed at God's command, that what we now see did not come from anything that can be seen* (NLT).

The quickening anointing take us out from under the depressing thought that our bodies, our dreams, and our destinies are as good as dead, and that God is making a mockery out of our lives and will never bring our promises to pass. It releases a sudden strengthening of faith that immediately shifts us out of thinking that all is dead. Suddenly, we feel life. Abraham felt this quickening anointing. And his wife, after picking herself up off the floor in a fit of laughter, got the anointing, too. Romans 4:18-20 tells us what the quickening anointing did for Abraham:

> Against all hope, Abraham in hope believed and so became the father of many nations, just as it had been said to him, "So shall your offspring be." Without weakening in his faith, he faced the fact that his body was as good as dead—since he was about a hundred years old—and that Sarah's womb was also dead. Yet he did not waver through unbelief regarding the promise of God, but was strengthened in his faith and gave glory to God.

In that moment of the impartation of quickening faith, Abraham felt something stirring. He didn't need Viagra®. Sarah, his wife, laughed because she knew she was in for some fun, and it had been so long since she was able to romp freely, youthfully in her spirit, soul, and body. The quickening anointing released a youthful vision, zeal, and energy that brought nations into existence and changed the world.

The quickening anointing is for the young and the old. Young Timothy felt it and talked about it in First Timothy 1:14:

> The grace of our Lord was poured out on me abundantly, along with the faith and love that are in Christ Jesus.

Timothy received a grace and an anointing to preach. Old men despised his youth because he was fresh and vibrant and moved in power and wisdom, and they had lost it (see 1 Tim. 4:12). They needed the quickening that Abraham got; yet it was easier for them to despise youthfulness than seek God for a quickening anointing that would move them into a new phase of ministry.

Grace, faith, and love—the three components of the anointing that quickens the power of God in us—are ours for the asking.

Timothy also knew that there is something that aborts vision and purpose. We can spontaneously miscarry the anointing if we are careless. If our conscience convicts us of something, we can shipwreck or abort our faith, walk away from our anointing, lay down our gifts, and hide (see 1 Tim. 1:19).

If we willingly follow deceiving spirits, bow down to the Baal worship of our culture (drugs, sex, pornography, materialism), or get caught up in a religious spirit, we are also in danger of miscarrying the anointing (see 1 Tim. 4:1).

But there is a remedy, a preparation to receive a greater vision and quickening anointing than ever before. It is the blood of Christ that we need to appropriate over and over again, cleansing us from a guilty conscience, renewing our faith, and opening us up to such a deep, deep sense of His love that we become close and intimate with Him once again and receive an impartation of anointing—a quickening anointing—that will excite us to persevere with joy and carry to term what He has formed within our world.

The Lord is calling us back to the Holy Place, through the blood of Jesus.

> *Therefore, brothers and sisters, since we have confidence to enter the Most Holy Place by the blood of Jesus...let us draw near to God with a sincere heart in full assurance of faith having our hearts sprinkled to cleanse us from a guilty conscience and having our bodies washed with pure water* (Hebrews 10:19,22 TNIV).

Jesus knows what you have been through and where you have been, and He is calling you back into the embrace of His mercy, so that He can re-anoint you with His presence:

*So then, since we have a great High Priest who has entered heaven, Jesus the Son of God, let us hold firmly to what we believe. This High Priest of ours understands our weaknesses, for He faced all of the same testings we do, yet He did not sin. So let us come boldly to the throne of our gracious God. There we will receive His mercy, and we will find grace to help us when we need it most* (Hebrews 4:14-16 NLT).

But what happens when you cannot seem to get back to that place with Him? He comes after us.

Each of those three visions I received of Jesus over the years drew me closer to Him after a time of drifting away from my faith. Each one drew me closer to receiving the quickening anointing. The first released me from my tendency to spontaneously abort or sabotage His purpose and destiny in me. I would become pregnant with vision but could not carry it to term because of the pain in my life. I needed an encounter with Him to enable me to move on. The second vision of Jesus freed me from fear, guilt, and shame and prepared me for deeper intimacy with Him. The third vision of Christ released the quickening anointing that changed my life and catapulted me into my destiny.

All three revealed the power of the cross and the blood—the atonement that we need to receive in order to become one with Him. We all need healing to receive the love of God, to become pregnant with vision, destiny, and gifts, and to make it to the time of quickening and to receive the crowns that the Lord Himself will place upon our heads.

God has set you on a path of sacred destiny. You have probably experienced moments when you tried to abort your anointing but didn't, much to the delight of the Father. Even if you did, God is in the process of restoring your anointing. There is more to come!

Chapter Five

# FROM BURNING ONE
# TO BURNING OUT

She sat slumped in her chair like a big, round beach ball in the process of deflating, the life drained from her eyes. Usually vibrant and alive, this woman's state shocked me. I was deeply glad that she had come to my burnout recovery workshop for pastors and leaders. I spent some time between sessions ministering to this woman who had been in very visible, very powerful prophetic ministry for years. The years had taken their toll. Tears welled up in her eyes as she talked about how tired she was, her own needs going unmet under the demands of international ministry.

I said, "You have got to unplug for awhile. You cannot stand with one hand plugged into the light socket of God's power and the other hand stretched out to the light socket of the demands of people constantly pulling on you. Nobody is meant to withstand that. You need to rest."

She was too far gone to hear me. I missed the degree of her burnout and missed the opportunity of helping her figure out a plan to shift the load of ministry and take time to address the unmet needs that were screaming for attention. She ended up in such a vulnerable place that she took a lover and moved away from her church, her calling, and the respect that she had built up over the years.

It happens all the time. The most common cause of people leaving a line of work, or the ministry, is burnout. The second most common reason why people leave the ministry in particular is moral failure. Guess what precedes moral failure? In the absence of some sexual compulsion or addiction, burnout is the precursor to moral failure. Many pastors and leaders subconsciously seek a way out of their ministries, so they sabotage themselves during a state of burnout and fall into sexual sin. But the root issues are related to the emotional and spiritual state of depletion we call *burnout*.

Parents burn out all the time as they become emotionally fatigued. Young moms find the incessant demands of toddlers overwhelming at times. Older parents burn out in their struggle with teenage rebellion. Businessmen and women burn out as their workloads increase and their support decreases, or their jobs become so routine that they are lulled into numbness and a rut they cannot break free from. Those in the helping professions often suffer from a state of burnout called "compassion fatigue." I heard one pastor, who worked as a counselor, jokingly tell me that when someone came up to him to talk about counseling issues in church, he wanted to reply, "Here is a quarter—call someone who cares." That is compassion fatigue.

Young and zealous for God, many run full on into full-time ministry pastoring American churches, launching ministries, or venturing off in missions. Years later, most discover that burnout has taken its toll, and help either never came, or they didn't know where to turn. Marriages crumble, kids turn away, tempers flare, criticism increases, lies and attacks demolish inner reserves, drugs and alcohol numb the pain, and pornography or affairs offer a tantalizing respite from reality. Perhaps you are one of the 1500 people who leave the ministry every month. You've gone from *burning one*—full of the fire of God's anointing, to burning out.

The symptoms include cynicism, anger, depression and physical symptoms such as ongoing headaches and stomachaches. Some burnout victims become critical, irritable, or withdrawn. These are just some of the symptoms of burnout.

The causes of burnout are more complex. Some feel like they have no control over the outcomes of their work. Others feel like the perceived demands on them outweigh their external support systems. Interpersonal conflicts and ongoing encounters with toxic people who criticize, often viciously, or who work to split key relationships and turn parties against one another can also hasten burnout.

There are many causes for burnout. Uncovering the triggers in your personal life will enable you to prevent burnout, or at least ecognize how you can start the recovery process.

So what now?

Burnout happens. But restoration also happens—if you let it. Let's look at one leader's rise and fall and the lessons he learned about the anointing along the way. By the end of the story, I believe we will all come to see what marks one who will make it to the end, what we need to finish well, and how we can all help each other enter into the fullness of Christ and reach our destinies.

Carl Tuttle was part of the core leadership team of the Vineyard Movement pastored by the late John Wimber. Carl talks about the progression of his ministry—a ministry that began as a young teenager leading Bible studies for other kids in his hurch. Ministry eventually took Carl into leading worship in one of the hottest churches of its era, and to teaching and playing internationally at huge conferences. Finally, it led him into planting a successful church before being called back to lead the Anaheim Vineyard in the waning years of John Wimber's ministry.

Carl talks about his descent into burnout as the pressures of shouldering the load of the Anaheim Vineyard took its toll. He also talks about the long process of recovery. The following is an excerpt from an interview with Carl.

**Before John Wimber passed away, you were the one who was called to lead the Anaheim, California, church, and then it wasn't long before you stepped down from leadership. Can you talk about the reasons why and the pressures that you experienced?**

I had a church in Santa Maria that I planted in 1984, and then in 1990 I came back to Anaheim to assist John and to join the staff as one of his many assistants. But my desire was to come alongside him. I knew he was under a lot of pressure and lots of strain, and I felt like the Lord was saying to go back and serve God's purposes in John, to set aside my own purposes and call and serve God's purposes in John. So it was two and a half years maybe into that that John had cancer and had to step back from ministry. He appointed me the lead guy. So I was basically running things and coordinating the preaching, and preaching some myself, and it was a lot of pressure.

Sometimes I got more out of it than I should have. God was giving me lots of visibility, authority, favor, and lots of influence. I think I misused it in that I think I tried to fill that place in my heart that just belonged to Him with those things. So ministry became my identity, my authority became my identity, my influence became my identity, and my success became my identity. I think those things are vapors. They can't do what God is meant to do. We are meant to find our identity in Him.

John asked me to take the church, saying that God had told him 54 times that I was supposed to take the church. I tried to leave at one point, and he came to me and said if I left I would be leaving my inheritance. So I felt like I really had no choice but to take the church. I didn't want any part of it. I didn't want to follow John Wimber. When I realized it was inevitable, I think I went manic and just started paddling as hard as I could to try to keep above water. Within two and a half years, I was completely and totally burnt out and hit the wall and began to isolate and withdraw and find refuge in myself. I was just gone.

## Did anybody recognize that?

Well, evidently not. I did. That is what was astounding to me. I was telling people that I wasn't making it. I was having panic attacks and being taken to the hospital; I was popping Valium® in the middle of staff meetings, right in front of everybody. I had told them that my marriage wasn't making it. Sonya and I said right in front of the pastors and their wives and interns, "We are not making it." I said, "I don't feel like I'm qualified to be head elder of this church."

Nobody seemed to hear any of it. I sat down on the steps of church on a Sunday night and just said I wasn't making it. I confessed to the whole Southern California pastoral prayer meeting that I was feeling drawn and seduced by alluring spirits and confessed that in front of these pastors and my own staff.

Then I hit the wall. My wife and I had a big blowout in July 1997, and when that happened, I was ready to step back. I met with Todd Hunter, John and Carol Wimber, and others, and I just willingly stepped down. Everyone seemed to be caught by surprise, and I never understood how they could be so surprised when I was so clear that I wasn't making it. So I don't know what that was.

## So you stepped out and the backlash wasn't pleasant.

I stepped down in July of 1997 and it was really funny—for years people thought I wanted back. But I was done, done, done. I wanted to see our marriage restored, our family restored. That was all I really wanted, I did not expect to be cut off and ostracized and exiled to the level that I was. That caught me very much by surprise. That was very difficult for me to handle, and it was very difficult for me to recover from.

## It's very strange when the church that professes to be more of a hospital turns around and shoots the wounded.

Yeah, there was never any sense of anyone coming alongside. There was never any sense of help. Everything that came was from outside, and it's OK. God more than took care of me. It just wasn't from the means and places, and people I thought it would come from. I thought the people I had met when I was a little boy and had grown up in ministry with through all of this, would come alongside us and say, "Gosh, they're in trouble; we need to help them." But instead, I received real anger and hostility and disappointment. It was really stunning to me, and I didn't know what to do with it all.

## What did you do?

I got very, very, very depressed. I think that is what ultimately destroyed our marriage. We did get back together after 18-20 months of separation, counseling, and we are doing OK, but I think I didn't really handle the rejection and the loss of all that took place. I was just in a dark hole for a long, long time.

## It is extremely hard to live with a depressed spouse.

Sonya said, or actually I asked her, "If you didn't have to be married to me, would you be?" She said, "No." And then I said, "Well, you don't have to be." I really couldn't blame her for not wanting to be hitched to my wagon; there were just so many ups and so many downs. I was so hooked by this whole thing that had taken place and wasn't able to let go of it. I'd try a new approach, and I couldn't understand how the people that I had known all my life, and others that I had known and grown close to over the years in college and ministry, could become so dis-attached and sometimes so hard toward me. I didn't understand what I had done that had been so egregious. I hadn't had an affair; I hadn't done any of the typical things that would disqualify somebody. It was just different.

## So tell me, how did you begin to recover?

It was interesting. In March of 2005, I moved from Fort Collins, Colorado, to Palm Desert, California, and I did so to find work. I had had a record label, a worship label after Vineyard, and I had done consulting after that and all that dried up in 2005, and so I fell back into construction. So I went to Southern California to paint and to work, and in that process I was very, very isolated. There were some people I was in contact with, but I wouldn't spend time with anybody.

And then one day in October, I got a phone call from a couple that had been very close to Sonya and me. They were in Calvary Chapel Yorba Linda with us in 1978. So I get this phone call and I find out they lived in the desert and they wanted to get together. I really liked them a lot and hadn't been connected in years and years, so I went over to their house and had dinner, and we talked, and we laughed, and we cried, and we just did that for weeks and weeks.

Then at some point they said "Where do you go to church?" And I said, "I don't go to church." They said, "If you did, where would you go?" And I said, "I wouldn't. I don't know... I don't know what to tell you." They said, "You don't know any place?" I said, "Well, there's this little church that meets, and we could go there."

So we went to this little church, and to me it was just awful, but they liked it. So later, he and I were out after church playing golf; he belonged to a country club and so he took me out to play golf. I hadn't played golf in years because, frankly, I couldn't afford to and couldn't afford the time either. I remember standing on the tenth tee, and he said, "Well, why don't you lead worship at that church?" I said, "They really need to ask you. It's like am I going to come in and say, 'Here I am!'"

A couple of weeks later, I get a call from the senior pastor and he asks me what I am doing in town, and if I was going to be around, and would I be interested in leading worship for them. I said, "No, I wouldn't. I paint all the time, and sometimes I have jobs on Sunday, and I really can't afford it not to be at work."

He said, "We will pay you a salary." And they ended up offering me enough that it made it worth my while. I was fully honest with everyone; I took that job as a mercenary. I had no interest in being involved with the people or the church; I just got up and led worship and left.

**But it's like the anointing breaks the yoke; you step back into the anointing and it breaks everything off.**

Yeah, well, for me worship is where I connect. And so it forced me into being connected and then I noticed something really curious about this little group of people—nobody asked me anything. Nobody asked if I was married, nobody asked if I was an ax murderer; they didn't seem to stick their noses in my business in any way, shape, or form. They just kept telling me how much they appreciated me, and affirmed me, loved me, accepted me. Over time, I got more involved and began to lead outreach and do all kinds of stuff. Then one day I said, "Oh my gosh, these people have healed me." By their love and acceptance, something had changed. It was just a wonderful thing.

It is not a church that you would consider "Spirit-filled." It must have been 2006 by the time I started leading worship on a regular basis, so in the four years I've been there, it wasn't until six months ago that the Holy Spirit was even mentioned. So there was little expectation of God doing anything, and it was killing me; it was killing me. A few months ago, the lead pastor got filled with the Spirit in a wonderful way and what we are experiencing now reminds me of what we were experiencing in my sister's living room in the days before we headed into the Vineyard movement. It was so sweet, and it was so fresh and so gentle, and everyone is being drawn into it in a marvelous way.

**So where do you go from here? What's God speaking to you?**

I work part time at the church and paint the other part time. People are really kind to me, and I love Facebook because people from around the world that I've known the last 40 something years, have all reached out to me at times and been very affirming, and it really is edifying. But this thought came to me—I really don't want to be known for who I was and for what I did. I want to be known for who I am and what I am doing today. I came to Christ 45 years ago. I've had this incredible breadth of experience, whether it be church planting, or worship leading, or leading a camp, or leading a high school group, or teaching Sunday school, or whatever it is. I'm hoping God will take all this life experience, and whatever gifts and talents He has given me, and take this last season of my life and just invest and make deposits wherever He will allow me to.

## Where do you think God is taking the Church in the coming years?

I don't know. The Church is so diverse and so divided, and that's OK, but we have to deal with that. There are so many different streams and each feels like it knows what God is doing in these next few years. When I hear them, I just kind of shrug, because I remember what they said God was going to do over the last 15 years, and it's not happened. I would just hope the very same thing that John Wimber was saying back in 1982, that the Holy Spirit wants His Church back, will happen. That's my hope, that the Church would be empowered and enabled to do the work of God versus all this other silly stuff we do that we say is the work of God.

## And what is the work of God? What is the anointing for?

To preach to the captives, and to minister to the poor and care for the needy, and demonstrate God's compassion and mercy for those around us. So it's expressing His love and compassion in every situation that we can. It's one person at a time and hopefully that grows.

**It's almost like you are right back at the beginning, back to the small-group, sweetness of God's presence and relationship. It's like He doesn't ever want us to leave that.**

> I am involved in one of the richest, most wonderful small groups. I've always had small groups over the years. I've probably had ahalf dozen different ones that have melded together, and I am in the midst of one now where lives have been joined together in such a marvelous and wonderful way, and there is ministry to one another, and out of that has come ministry to people outside of our group, to people at work. It's just awesome, and I don't know what's better than that. We keep trying to do all this other stuff, but I don't know what's better than knowing and being known [by God], and being loved and accepted—it's just as good as it gets.[1]

## How to Make It to the End

When you read Carl's story, you see several themes breaking through that are common experiences in the lives of those who burn out in ministry and crumble under the pressures of life. He talks about a perceived lack of support, increasing drug use to numb the pain and escape from the situation, escalating relationship problems with staff and peers, turning his pain and anger against the one closest to him (his wife), and finally, isolating and turning his back on all ministry and church involvement. Somewhere along the descent into madness, Carl's slide could have been arrested. Perhaps God intervened many times, but His interventions were shunned or ignored by Carl or by the staff of his church.

If you read Carl's story carefully, he revealed several key points where burnout could have been prevented…if only others had listened, they could have helped give him the permission he needed to step back and recover.

How do you intervene in the life of one who is burning out? Tough love calls for a time-out if needed. Some may just need to redirect their gifts into a more suitable expression of ministry. A pastor may need to let go of counseling and focus on teaching. He may need to realize that he is called to a more apostolic ministry. It may be time to break through the limitations of serving a single church and focus more regionally, or expand into international ministry. Both too much responsibility and too little challenge can precede burnout. The key to prevention is giving yourself permission to change according to the season of life you are in or according to the direction in which God is moving you.

What follows are some keys to endurance that others have found helpful:

1. Rest is a weapon of warfare. Most people in ministry burn out because they feel like they have to meet everyone's needs. We are not God. God has called us not just to minister, but also to enjoy Him, to enjoy relationships with those closest to us, and to love life.

2. Run away *to* Jesus; don't just run away. Secret anointing and hiddenness enables you to go deeper and abide with Jesus and prepares you for a greater platform that may only last for a season. At the end of that season, you have no need to make it continue because you have learned to be satisfied with Jesus and know who you are to Him. If it does continue, your secret history of deepening relationship with God will help you maintain the humility you need to sustain a highly visible ministry.

3. Criticism is inevitable but does not determine your self-worth. The judgmental attitude of many professing Christians is not the heart of God toward you. Preventing burnout requires you to understand that sometimes overly critical people have personality that can have a destructive impact on church groups. It's vital that you know how to protect yourself and how to create a healthy environment around you—a culture of honor rather than a culture of negativity.

4. When your love needs are being met through loving relationships, this releases the joy and provides the safe place you need to nurture and sustain yourself. Successful men and women in ministry often have type A, driven personalities. Their zeal and anointing open doors around the world and yet, as their energy wanes later in life, these same ministers realize that the most important focus of their lives has changed from God and ministry to deepening friendships and family ties. Love sustains us. Pouring our lives into a few ensures the transference of our anointing to the next generation. Our lineage becomes our legacy.

5. Working within the boundaries of your anointing will keep your energy focused. We all have a gift mix comprised of natural and spiritual gifts. Some gifts are more dominant during some seasons of life and ministry while others take a backseat. Staying in the flow of favor and doing what God is blessing will keep you from burning out and will ensure success. Trying to make something else happen, because that is who you want to be or what you want to do, sets you up for disappointment and burnout.

6. Focusing on Jesus and developing your own spiritual core, rather than trying to make your mission and mandate come to pass, will ensure that it comes to pass. There is a

reason why people take sabbaticals every seven years. It is because new gifts emerge at different ages in life. You need time to transition from one to the other. There is a reason why soldiers come off the battlefield and move to the rear detachment. It is because they need to rest and recover. No one can remain alert, or in a state of the adrenaline rush that accompanies war or ministry, for long. The victory is the Lord's. The Church belongs to Him. Don't try to hold on to something He is asking you to let go of.

7. Understand that friction or tension precedes breakthrough. Inner discomfort may be God prompting you to launch out in a different direction. Paying attention to that and praying into it (along with others who intercede for you) will enable you to make the transition into the new expression of anointing that God is calling you to. The calling on your life, or the way you worked and ministered in your 20s should look very different from the calling in your life and the way you work or minister as you approach 50.

8. Recognizing when it is time to shift out of one area of work or ministry and into another one will enable you to recover as you continue on. Oswald Chambers wanted to be an artist but realized God was calling him to be a great preacher. The great painter Van Gogh was a preacher among miners for a time before he discovered his anointing and destiny as an artist. The Creator is a creative God who invites you to tap into His creativity and express it in new ways that are uniquely you.

## Sealed With a Kiss

David burned out. Elijah burned out. Many key leaders in biblical history burned out. But they have one thing in common that enabled them to continue following God and fulfilling God's plans and purposes for their generation—they were sealed with a kiss, and they knew it. We are, too.

> *Now it is God who makes both us and you stand firm in Christ. He anointed us, set His seal of ownership on us, and put His Spirit in our hearts as a deposit, guaranteeing what is to come* (2 Corinthians 1:21-22).

The seal was historically used for different purposes: to mark a person's property, to secure his treasures, or to authenticate a deed. In the first sense, the Spirit marks us as His own, separating us unto Him. In the second sense of the use of a seal, He guards us and keeps watch over us as His precious jewels. In the third sense of the seal, He confirms or ratifies our title to salvation and our inheritance. Being aware that we are sealed releases a sense of security for the future. The Holy Spirit is the deposit in our lives that guarantees our heavenly inheritance, and what He has begun in our spirit and soul will be perfected in Heaven. We are living in the middle of eternity. Once we gain an eternal perspective, we can begin to relax our efforts and become secure in God's anointing and commission in our lives.

Watchman Nee, a turn-of-the-century Chinese preacher and author of great depth, knew burnout and the heavy weight of discouragement that almost caused him to become ashamed of serving the Lord for so many years without personal gain. At one point, he wrote about an encounter with a man that flung the condemnation of a materialistic culture into his face like dirt. At that moment, Nee sensed the seal upon his life. Suddenly, he was filled with the glory of God that shattered his discouragement. In that moment, he was sealed with a kiss from God:

> In 1929 I returned from Shanghai to my home town of Foochow. One day I was walking along the street with a stick, very weak and in broken health, and I met one of my old college professors. He took me into a teashop where we

sat down. He looked at me from head to foot and from foot to head, and then he said: "Now look here; during your college days we thought a good deal of you and we had hopes that you would achieve something great. *Do you mean to tell me that this is what you are?*" Looking at me with penetrating eyes, he asked that very pointed question. I must confess that, on hearing it, my first desire was to break down and weep. My career, my health, everything had gone, and here was my old professor who taught me law in the school, asking me: "Are you still in this condition, with no success, no progress, nothing to show?"

But the very next moment—and I have to admit that in all my life it was the first time—I really knew what it meant to have the "Spirit of glory" resting upon me. The thought of being able to pour out my life for my Lord flooded my soul with glory. Nothing short of the Spirit of glory was on me then. I could look up and without a reservation say, "Lord, I praise Thee! This is the best thing possible; it is the right course that I have chosen!" To my professor it seemed a total waste to serve the Lord; but that is what the Gospel is for—to bring us to a true estimate of his worth.

Judas felt it a waste. We could manage better with the money by using it in some other way. There are plenty of poor people. Why not rather give it for charity, do some social service for their uplift, help the poor in some practical way? Why pour it out at the feet of Jesus? (see John 12:4-6.) That is always the way the world reasons. "...Can you not do something better with yourself than this? It is going a bit too far to give yourself altogether to the Lord!"

But if the Lord is worthy, then how can it be a waste? He is worthy to be so served. He is worthy for me to be His prisoner. He is worthy for me just to live for Him. *He is worthy!* What the world says about this does not matter. The Lord says: "Do not trouble her." So let us not be troubled. Men may say what they like, but we can stand on this ground, that the Lord said: "It is a good work. Every true work is not done on the poor; every true work is done to me." When once our eyes have been opened to the real worth of our Lord Jesus, nothing is too good for Him.[2]

Ask the Lord to enable you to stand firm in Christ and resist burnout, and He will. Ask Him to show you how to enter into His rest and rest as you go—and He will. Ask for wisdom and strategy, fresh fire, a quickening anointing on your life that will fan the smoldering wick of your lampstand into a raging flame that cannot be hidden— and He will. Ask for more of the Holy Spirit. It is a prayer He delights to answer:

> So I say to you: Ask and it will be given to you; seek and you will find; knock and the door will be opened to you. For everyone who asks receives; he who seeks finds; and to him who knocks, the door will be opened.…If you then, though you are evil, know how to give good gifts to your children, how much more will your Father in heaven give the Holy Spirit to those who ask Him! (Luke 11:9-10, 13).

Ask away! And step out of your discouragement to reach out and receive. What is to come is way different from what we see now. Remember, you are His. You are sealed with a kiss. He values you too much to let you drown.

## Endnote

2. Watchman Nee, *The Normal Christian Life* (Carol Stream, IL: Tyndale House Publishers, 1977), 278-280, *http://books.google. com/books?id=091Cgt1MqXwC&printsec=frontcover&dq=a+n ormal+christian+life&cd=1#v=onepage&q=In%201929&f=false* (accessed November 30, 2011).

Chapter Six

# RESTORING THE ANOINTING

"Has he repented?" a man asked me when I told him I was giving some editorial advice to a leader who had fallen into disgrace and was making a comeback on the international ministry scene.

"Is it really any of our business?" I replied. "How could we ever judge whether someone has truly come back into the mindset of Christ and no longer seems enslaved to the things of this world?"

"But I heard he didn't follow through on his restoration process," the man countered, not to be deterred.

"Perhaps he didn't follow the route others laid out for him. Perhaps he followed God's route. The point is not that we continue to judge him, but that we begin to receive him as a brother in Christ and honor who he is. Restoring the anointing of one who has fallen into sin is a two-way street. The fallen one needs to get up and we need to let him," I found myself replying.

But the conversation troubled me…as do all conversations do about the spiritual life and ministry of others. We are all in need of a savior and often in need of mercy. None of us qualifies to cast stones at others. None of us ever gets to see and hear the whole picture behind someone's life—the pressures, the political influences, the ministry agendas of those who seek to either help or destroy another, the history of someone's relationships or addictions.

The man we were talking about is Paul Cain, a man who some call a noted prophet, and others call the last of a long line of healing evangelists from the days of the Latter Rain Movement. Either way, he ministered in an anointing that is rarely, if ever, seen. In recent years, Paul was confronted about moral failures and asked to submit to a restoration process. His experience is like that of many other fallen leaders. They struggle for years until being exposed. Then, when all of Heaven should rush in with healing, all hell seems to break loose instead. The fallen leader ends up in a controversy storm of thunderous words and lightning quick judgments that center around the topic of "restoration."

According to J. Lee Grady in a *Charisma Magazine* article:

I believe restoration is a serious issue. If a leader makes moral or ethical mistakes that hurt other people, especially ones as serious as Cain made, then he needs serious accountability. That's not being harsh. The Bible says those in public ministry have a stricter standard.

Those who worked closest with Cain during the last decade say he hasn't taken the steps they prescribed. But a group of ministers in California who began ministering to Cain a few months ago say he is walking through a rigorous recovery process.

I pray the folks in California are right.

Cain's story is tragic. He was once involved in the healing revival of the 1950s. He disappeared from the scene for 25 years and re-emerged in the 1990s as a modern prophet who could read people's mail from the podium and even give their street addresses, supposedly by revelation from God. But his ministry ended in 2005 when he admitted publicly that he struggled with homosexuality and alcoholism for an extended period of time.

"I am guilty as I can be," he told *Charisma* in March 2005. "I am going for counseling. I am getting as much help as I can."[1]

As a Christian counselor, I find myself in frequent dialog with other counselors and pastors about fallen leaders and their restoration process—especially those who topple off highly visible platforms. No one seems to agree on what should be done with them. Nor should we; everyone is so unique that it takes a team to listen for God's plan for individual restoration. The goal is to reconnect that individual to a vibrant relationship with Jesus and bring healing to the issues of heart and mind that they have tripped over.

Healing is the by-product of the reconnection of head and heart with the Holy Spirit. It can only take place in an atmosphere where the individual feels safe, loved, and accepted. Forced referrals and programs often do not work in the immediate aftermath of someone's addictions and moral failures coming to light. Defensiveness and lies scurry about like shadows running from the light that seeks to totally expose all that lies in darkness. It takes time for a person to even begin to be willing to enter a restoration process—especially if denial is strong or the ones who confront seem punitive in their approach. Often, the initial counselor or program may help transition the person into a restoration process, but may not be the one God ordains to see the process through to the end...if there is an end.

## What Is Restoration?

Many roads lead to destruction, but the way back is unpaved and unmapped. Independent churches usually have no plan in place or protocol acknowledged to handle the fallout of a minister's fall from grace. Shocked and embarrassed, the board members often react in judgment rather than love. One church may seek to kick the minister out, dismissing him quietly. Another church may try to punish and humiliate the "offender" on his way out the door. The minister ends up feeling abandoned, hurt, and betrayed by the barrage of abusive, caustic words hurled like stones from the lips of his brothers and sisters.

Those who offer the fallen leader some formal restoration process line him up with counselors for a predetermined length of time, according to the issue. Someone who has had an affair with a church secretary may fall into one category of formal restoration process; a practicing homosexual with multiple partners may fall into another category; and a pedophile still another.

One of the most dominant sexual sins rampant among leaders and followers of Christ seems to be pornography. The use of pornography is seen as a "victimless crime" that is not often taken seriously and usually receives little or no attention by the church board even if it does come to light. Those who take it seriously understand the implications of its use and realize just how much the use of porn impacts not only the minister, but also his family and the atmosphere of the church.

The Web site safefamilies.org offers a long list of chilling statistics about the use of pornography. Just the following statistics I gleaned gives us a clue as to why the Church is so weak.

- A 1996 Promise Keepers survey at one of their stadium events revealed that over 50% of the men in attendance were involved with pornography within one week of attending the event.

- 57% of pastors say that addiction to pornography is the most sexually damaging issue to their congregation (Christians and Sex Leadership Journal Survey, March 2005).

- Adults admitting to Internet sexual addiction: 10%; 28% of those are women.

- More than 70% of men from 18 to 34 visit a pornographic site in a typical month.

Millions of men in the U.S. and around the world are hooked on pornography. Often, they step into the world of prostitutes as a result of their escalating appetite for sensory pleasure and adventure. If they claim to be Christians, the guilt and shame often cause them to isolate. When the presence of God comes in power, these men will often shrink back and slink away, forfeiting the grace that could be theirs. How many of them were once called to extraordinary ministries? Many have lost their anointing due to their sexual confusion and addictions. Many others don't even try to step into their sacred destinies—they cannot when their eyes are hooked on other images.

One denomination has a defined restoration process for pastors and ministers who admit to the use of pornography. Its counseling guidelines are based on the "level" of pornography use. Those guidelines are as follows:

- Curiosity: requires three months professional counseling.

- Experimental: requires six months professional counseling.

- Regular: requires one year professional counseling and a three-month suspension of credentials.

- Habitual: requires one year professional counseling and a six-month suspension of credentials.

- Addictive: requires two years of professional counseling.

Does counseling work? It depends on the motivation of the counselee. Some are so wounded by the shame and feelings of being punished that they reject the process and disappear altogether. Others may not feel connected to the appointed counselor and may need to take a break, step back from church involvement, and ask God to lead them to the ones who can help. They are simply not ready or need to find someone they feel comfortable relating to before they can be ready to accept the process of accountability.

My experience in talking with anyone who has once walked with Jesus and then fallen into sexual sin—particularly the chronic use of pornography or a one-time adulterous situation (heterosexual or homosexual)—is that you can tell who is going to make progress and enter into freedom through formal counseling fairly quickly. Those who make the best progress display a broken and contrite spirit. They realize that they crossed biblical, ethical, and moral boundaries. They understand that something within them needs healing, and they want to be healed. And they also recognize how their actions have hurt those closest to them. Along the way, they willingly try to reconcile their relationships and come into an even deeper understanding of the trust issues between themselves and the Lord, as well as between themselves and the members of the church. They know that the issues of restoration are issues of relationships. It is one thing to try to get to the root of the sin in a person's life; it is quite another to reveal the fruit that sprang from his or her "earthiness."

The ones who resist the restoration process are initially defensive and angry that they got caught. Many will not admit to having done anything wrong. They will shift the blame to others, and remain bitter and angry toward other Christians and leaders who "ousted" them.

They flee the process that has been scripted for them and walk their own paths for awhile, deciding when and if they want to submit to a restoration process.

Then there are those who acknowledge that they have crossed the boundary line, yet choose to flow with the river that leads away from God. Many choose to divorce and move in with their lovers. Or they find another community that accepts their addictions or sexual compulsions and normalizes them. Eventually, they may take the slow boat back as the affair ends, the lover leaves, the burnout subsides, and they come to their senses and wander back into the church, looking for God.

That takes courage. The ones who say it is better to be a door-keeper in the house of the Lord than to sit outside partying with sinners are ones who have become broken and contrite and are more than ready for restoration.

All of these fallen believers have been through hell. What they need is grace and love. Understanding, compassion, and forgiveness are the three keys to helping restore someone. First, the person must feel accepted in order for correction to be received. For any restoration process to be successful, the goals need to be clear. Restoration is about restoring the individual to a vibrant relationship with the Lord. It is not about getting him or her back into the pulpit or on the road as itinerant ministers.

## Counting Sins

God does not count men's sins against them. Restoration is not about counting sins.

*All this is from God, who reconciled us to Himself through Christ and gave us the ministry of reconciliation: that God was reconciling the world to Himself in Christ, not counting men's sins against*

*them. And He has committed to us the message of reconciliation*
(2 Corinthians 5:18-19).

Too often, we believe that we should bring a person to repentance, when God is asking us to bring the person into reconciliation. "God was reconciling to Himself." God is the initiator, not the recipient, of reconciliation. Jesus paid the debt and cancelled out our sins on the cross. How many of them? Can you count yours? Can I count mine? Do you know the sins of omission or just the sins of commission?

To the Greek, *paraptomata* (the word translated "sins" in First Corinthians 5:19), can be mistakes that result from ignorance, false steps, "slips," or "whoops" moments.[6] To the Jew, sins and trespasses are deliberate actions knowingly committed against God. According to the apostle Paul, we are called to be ministers of reconciliation, assisting people to receive forgiveness—not meting out punishments.

Restoration, then, is a process of assisting a person to realize and receive what God has done for him or her on the cross. Counseling apart from an understanding of the blood of Jesus and the cross of Christ is fruitless. Restoration is not about punishment of the "offender." Nor is it about doing damage control in the church. Punishment does not work. Love does. God is near to the brokenhearted. Get people in touch with their broken heart and they will find the presence of God as a welcome friend.

## Restoring Trust

Too often church leaders focus on the one who fell, but he or she is not the only one who needs to be restored. This fallen believer's spouse and family also need tender care. Members of the church are hurting, too. Trust has been shattered. Before forgiveness ensues and trust can be restored, church members need to understand the complexity of issues smoldering under the surface that contributed to their leader's fall. Initial meetings help, but only if they focus on gaining insight and understanding and allow time to help people process the event. One way to do this is by offering a "critical incident debriefing."

I've conducted many "critical incident debriefings" as a counselor. If done correctly, they help with damage control and mitigate against ongoing trauma. They also help identify those who need more individual help. I've debriefed parent groups in the aftermath of a leader being arrested for child abuse and walked with them through the complex emotions and fears they have for their children. I've also counseled with the children who looked up to their teacher and now were obsessed with some aspect of the case, or were dealing with an unreasonable fear. I've debriefed clergy and churches in the aftermath of suicide and know that while restoration of the deceased was not possible, many people impacted by the suicide needed to be restored in some way. I've also conducted Burnout Recovery workshops for pastors and leaders and given them the tools they need to prevent them from falling. Along the way, I have come to realize that some will make it past their feelings to the point of forgiveness, and some won't.

## What Restoration Protocol Should Be Established?

You can put guidelines in place to deal with situations that might arise; however, every situation is as different as the personality who perplexes everyone. Perhaps there needs to be a set of guidelines or protocols on how boards should deal with the fallen minister. Perhaps not. Dragging them into a public confession and kicking them out is not exactly the process of reconciliation that God has in mind. Laying out a series of hoops to jump through and hurdles to leap, can cause the fallen leader to feel punished, condemned, and isolated rather than loved and helped. Dictating a course of action could invite further rebellion.

Central to the process is helping the fallen to find reconciliation, peace, and the knowledge of God's love and forgiveness. This is important for the fallen, the family, and the church. To accomplish it, several questions need to be asked, and the answers need to involve the fallen leader. One who enters into a collaborative process of reconciliation will find himself restored in record time. Collaborative efforts draw people in and invite them to take the lead in their healing rather than feel like children being reprimanded and told what to do.

Here are some suggested questions that will help start and continue the process:

1. Is the issue a one-time thing, or is it ongoing?

2. What do you believe to be the underlying causes of your behavior?

3. Do you have the capacity of feeling empathy for all concerned and insight into how others are impacted?

4. Will you take responsibility to clean up the mess?

5. Do you need a break from ministry to recover from burnout or a prolonged absence to deal with mental illness or addictions?

6. How can we love you back into reconciliation with God?

7. How can we love your family and the church into forgiveness and restored relationships? How can we help all of you regain trust?

These are not questions that can be answered overnight. After the initial disclosure, strong feelings and defensive reactions are common. Anger and pain spews out. Eventually, as the feelings subside, the questions can be addressed during a series of meetings. Most people don't know what the issues are or what they need. Love and acceptance are needed to create a safe place for the person and his family to begin to explore the answers. It takes time. The collaborative process encourages the fallen leader to recognize the root issues in his life and take responsibility to mend not only himself, but those he hurt as well.

## Return to Ministry or Not?

Most reasonable people agree that there are some who should never be allowed to return to ministry. Convicted predatory sex offenders and pedophiles, for example, should never be allowed to work in positions that involve individual contact, for obvious reasons. The Catholic Church has had to deal with the issue of pedophiles for years. Where do these priests go after their sins have been exposed? In past history, they were simply moved to another parish where they continued to act out their sexual deviancy until someone stepped up and said enough was enough. Today, they are grappling with the difficult decisions on how to treat the sex offenders initially and then, if they are not in jail, where to place them afterward.

Clinical counselors have long recognized that men often come to God to manage their addictions and predatory behaviors. The pastoral role is often used by clergy in an attempt to manage their sexual addictions, deny their existence, and minimize the consequences both to themselves and to victims. Their loneliness, over-identification with their role as a "minister," and the lack of rewarding personal relationships cause them to perpetuate the cycle and enable them to maintain secrets. Those who are struggling with sexual addictions need extensive help. Depending on the type of sexual addiction, some should never be restored to public ministry.

For some, it seems like the presence and power of God are not enough to help them rein in their passions and compulsions. Redemption, forgiveness, and healing are always possible but often not probable for many reasons. Either properly trained counselors are unavailable, or unknown, or they cannot follow through on the long process of healing that includes rebuilding the foundation of the fallen person's personality from the ground up.

Those who should never be allowed back into positions of ministry also include those with severe personality disorders that have gone undiagnosed or untreated, particularly, pathological narcissists, those who use power without having any evident relationship with Jesus and manipulate others for their own personal gain. These people should be removed from ministry or prevented from returning. Their disorders prevent them from developing empathy, or valuing individuals the way Christ sees them. Pathological narcissists are incapable of personal reflection and are very threatened by anyone's criticism that might damage their own image of perfection.

Many gravitate toward ministry because they seek the admiration of the people, love the accolades, but have no ability to care for others beyond themselves. Many are either womanizers or promiscuous homosexuals. Severe narcissism is defined as a pervasive pattern of grandiosity, need for admiration, and lack of empathy. They are not the kind of pastors people want in their churches. They often gravitate to itinerant ministry; love the applause that comes with displays of power, signs, and wonders; and love the money they walk away with. Severe narcissists are more in love with themselves than with God. They want to be bigger, better, and louder than anyone, as well as more admired, successful, and wealthier than any other. Their anointing may be powerful, but their authority is shaded by the shifting shadows within.

## Seven-Day Restorations

King Nebuchadnezzar spent seven years wallowing in the thick of mental illness and no one dared try to restore him during that time (see Dan. 4). For King David, however, it took seven days. David was not mentally ill; neither was he engaged in a pattern of narcissistic, predatory behavior, nor did he have a personality disorder. He was a normal man who eventually gave in to a sense that he was entitled to anything he wanted in life to meet his perceived unmet needs.

Many pastors hold up the story of King David as a model of restoration and cite Second Samuel 12 as the formula that one should follow during a time of restoration. The pattern started with David's open acknowledgment of failure and calling it like it was—murder and adultery, coveting and greed. After seven days of prayer and weeping, David accepted the fact that there were repercussions from his actions that could not be thwarted. He realized that he needed to clean up his mess, and accepted the fact that some things just could not be undone. By verse 20, we see David getting up from his shame and humility, washing himself of the condemnation and anointing himself with the oil of joy and gladness—despite feeling the opposite. The anointing enabled him to step back out into his authority. It was a time of re-commissioning and restoring his position. David changed his clothes, the fact which is symbolic of stepping back into his kingly authority. He worshiped and reconnected with God. Finally, in verses 24 and 25, David accepted what he could not change and extended mercy to others.

Some leaders believe that fallen leaders should just step right back into their positions of authority and ministry. They cite David's seven-day restoration as a model to be followed. However, seven days is more symbolic of a period of completion than an actual time frame that implies a fallen leader should just get right back into ministry.

David's process of restoration is common to warriors even today. He had to come back into his true personality humbly submitted to God, a personality that had become warped through the years by fighting one too many battles. David had to shift from a place of being a warrior to becoming a lover. His process of restoration enabled him to regain his position of sonship—a sonship that initiated his ascent to the kingship.

In my consulting work, I've worked with countless soldiers, predominantly male who find themselves undergoing a process of restoration after returning from the battlefields of Iraq and Afghanistan. They left the U.S. as lovers, fathers, husbands, and sons. They returned hardened, weary, suspicious, and often with a sense of feeling entitled to relieve the adrenaline rush of war through prostitutes or reckless behaviors and spousal abuse. They had to shift out of the warrior mentality, set aside the memories and intrusive images of battles, and return to becoming sons, lovers, and fathers. It was not an easy shift to make for many—especially since they knew they were going back downrange.

I've watched the faces of those who managed to navigate the restoration process. When they first returned, they were sun-baked and hard, gruff with their families, and unsure of themselves in civilian life. After a month or so, their faces softened and smiles returned. They were on their way to recovery, but it would take months to restore some sense of equilibrium in the family. Others were not so lucky and needed more time and professional help.

We see this same hardening of heart in many who fall in ministry or burnout, and walk away from ministry. True, biblical restoration is all about restoring the heart of the son or the daughter to the Father. It is about restoring the love of community. Restoring the anointing and one's spiritual authority is more tenuous, and it may or may not happen along the way.

Prophetic minister John Paul Jackson talks about the difficulty of using David as a model of restoration and about true biblical restoration from his point of view:

> I've known men and women who have made a comeback, but not a single one has ever came back as strong as before, let alone stronger. David never came back as strong as before

Bathsheba. When you fall, it is more than just a sin; the damage it does to family and those who follow is horrible.

When people say David was forgiven instantly and immediately put back into "ministry," I say they are confused. David who was a king, who could have multiple wives, was responsible for implementing God's desire for the kingdom as a whole and responsible for the safety of a people. Priests were responsible to minister to God from the position of the people. Prophets brought the desires of God to the people. Biblically, kings were allowed more than one wife, priests only one wife. People say, "David never stepped down from ministry after he fell," and I have to reply, "So you're advocating that priests and prophets can have more than one wife?"

A lack of character development will kill your influence. Failure to differentiate between power and authority will also kill the anointing. For example, you think you're OK 'cause the power is still flowing through you. However, power without relationship with Jesus is lawlessness. Authority is the fruit of a relationship with God. Authority comes only by relationship. In Matthew 7, people were saying didn't we do this and that…. And Jesus said, "Depart from me! You took ⅹ the gift and used it without ever knowing me."

To know the giver of the gift, to know the Father is to begin to move in true authority. The Bible doesn't say that the gifts and authority are given without repentance. The gifts and calling are given without repentance. God is saying, I'll not revoke the gifts and calling, but I'll also not endorse you. ⅹ Therefore, you see all these men and women who move in power but seem to have no authority.

The Church teaches that if you are gifted, you get a dispersion of grace. Grace then, mistakenly means covering the sin of the person because they still operate in power. Power is a gift that God will not take back. Call it "grace" and people believe that God will cover all our sin, so that you never have to repent of anything again. He died to forgive that sin but you frustrate grace when you don't repent from the sin. ✗

The key to restoring the anointing is this—are you going to repent or not? If you don't repent—you become defiled. Jesus said to the unrepentant ones, "I must go. We have nothing in common." Without repentance, you have something in common with the evil one—and that is called defilement.[2] ✗

## Perspectives on the Process of Restoration

Repentance is the beginning of restoration. ✗ It is making a decision to turn back, to change your mind about where you are going, and to start walking toward Jesus rather than away. It also implies that you have been suddenly made aware of the deception that had overtaken you. The blinders are off. The eyes of your understanding have opened and you see the result of your actions—and the impact on others. Godly sorrow fills your heart. But then, just as suddenly, God's loving presence and heart toward you commands you to stand up again. It is time to walk on into a deeper healing process and great anointing. After all, you have been sealed by the Holy Spirit. You are His. He is not about to let you go. And God will not leave you defiled by His archenemy.

John Paul Jackson elaborated on this view of what a restoration process should look like in an article he wrote called, "5 Phases of Restoration Process—Not Just Forgiveness."[3]

Obviously, I am not against restoration; I am against quick restoration. I believe that time is required. In my opinion, there are five phases fallen ministers must go through to successfully return to ministry. Each phase may take a year or longer.

X 1. First, they must recognize their sin and repent with deep-felt sorrow. They must realize what they have done—not only to their spouses but also to God. This takes time because there are layers of realization that must be worked through.

X 2. Second, they must find the root cause of the sin and eradicate it. I have never counseled anyone who fell the first time he or she was tempted. What causes them to dwell on the temptation? The answer usually lies in several issues, not just one, and again, it takes time to find them. The more we leave undiscovered, the more likely we are to commit that sin again.

X 3. Third, there must be additional time for the wound to heal. Think of it this way: We can pull out the knife, but the pain is still there, and the deeper the wound, the longer it will take to heal. The patient must become stable, or he or she will likely fall and be injured again.

X 4. Fourth, the men and women need to be tested. If there has been moral sin, we should watch how they handle themselves around the other sex. What sex do they gravitate toward? Where do they look, and where do they go as they mingle with others? There are many telltale signs of where people are in the restoration process, but they take time to discover, and as the person heals, the number of signs or habits becomes less.

X 5. Fifth, ministers in the restoration process should be given responsibility slowly, and we should observe how they handle it. Pride was the fall of satan, and it is the basis for the fall of humankind. Premature promotion will wipe out the brokenness and contrition that invite God to come near and continue the healing. In our drive to implement grace, we often seem to forget that Scripture says, *"The LORD is near to those who have a broken heart, and saves such as have a contrite spirit"* (Psalm 34:18 NKJV). It also says, *"The sacrifices of God are a broken spirit, a broken and a contrite heart—these, O God, You will not despise"* (Psalm 51:17 NKJV). This level of restoration can take as long as five years.[2]

The sense of urgency and fear of losing visibility leads many to cry out for instant restoration. Who has five to ten years to spare for a restoration process? This era of instant celebrity status via the Internet and television leads many young adults to seek instant celebrity ministry status as well. They want to be famous. Who has years to devote to the process of character development when talent—or *dunamis*—can rocket you to the top?

Many believe that restoration can take place more quickly, depending on the individual and the depth of his or her need. However, how quickly it happens depends on the individual's ability to embrace a process that includes healing, character development (cleaning up the mess), and submitting to limitations on further ministry.

Barbara Yoder, an apostle based in Ann Arbor, Michigan, who, alongside her husband, founded a thriving church called Shekinah, has been in ministry for many years. Having dealt with many broken people, she knows that different people need different approaches. The younger generation coming into ministry come from much more broken backgrounds and a permissive world culture that results in a different approach, one that enables them to heal as they continue to minister, but also tempers their desire for fame.

Discipline is necessary when people fall into certain types of sin. I've worked with them and had others work with them to help them get free. Discipline means to sit down and get what is causing them to get out of control, under control. If there is something inside of them that needs addressing, I know I've

got to get them into counseling on the side because I know
Xthat the trauma that isn't yet healed, or whatever the issue is,
will cause them to fall at a strategic time in their ministry.
But at the same time, I may let them minister because they
are not currently active in sin. I keep ministry limited until
there is a certain level of wholeness there because otherwise,
it will be setting them up for a fall. People need tough love X
and real love and if they have fallen, they need to submit to
it. Some people should never be put back into the ministry
position they were in.

This generation coming in is a mess. Do they need therapy,
deliverance, or what do these young ones need? Sometimes
I just minister to them and see if they can get free. That is
why we need the healing rooms, counseling rooms, and then
we need people who understand the problems and moms
and dads who will disciple these kids all the way through
to freedom. I'm really focused on helping people and leaders
experience God and develop in character. I've got our young
people connecting in prayer and in the Word. If they keep
in prayer, that is where they get transformed. When they are
right with God, they are powerful!!!![4]

## Restoration Is a Two-Way Street

We need to suspend judgment and release the healing love
that characterizes the nature of Jesus. The next outpouring of God
will likely break off all that hinders us—our own guilt and shame,
our judgments of others who have fallen or offended us or demolished us in some way—and fill us with a sense of real love and
power necessary for us to survive the coming years.

When that outpouring of unconditional love occurs, it will
rain on the just and the unjust alike. Some who have fallen in the
past will be raised up to a new level of power and anointing. The

wisdom they have gained in their restoration process may become the greatest qualifier of authority in the days to come, especially given the brokenness of the next generation, a generation who is largely fatherless and sexually ambiguous. Those who have fallen into sexual sin of any sort, whether homosexual or heterosexual, and walked through a genuine healing process, may be the ones most qualified to lead the next generation. Will we embrace the fullness of the restoration of their anointing—and then some?

## The Anointing to Unmask Baal

We can seek to restore individuals from now to the end of time; however, there is a larger problem facing us. It has to do with the spiritual influences, the shifting shadows that seek to obscure the light and entice men and women into darkness. Where are the leaders who realize that we fight not against flesh and blood but against a spiritual realm that seeks to enslave us and rob us from entering into the fullness of Christ? Where are the leaders who carry the anointing to release churches, and even cities, from the grip of Baal—the spirit behind greed and sexual perversion that is robbing thousands from their sacred destinies? The Church, as a whole, needs to be restored.

In the ancient days of Canaanite spirituality, the worship of Baal and Asherah, a pillar or image of wood was set up with the image of Baal and was worshiped with libidinous and lascivious practices. Originally, the idol was worshiped as a symbol of the tree of life, but later it was perverted to mean the origin of life and was pictured with the male organs of procreation (see Ezek. 16:17).

The worship of Baal eventually equated with the worship of the phallus as a symbol primarily of male generative power. With the worship of Asherah, the symbol sometimes changes to that of the female organ. Canaanites spread the images and sexual practices related to "fertility rites" to the rest of the world. Relics of it are found among all ancient civilizations. It led to the destruction of all Canaanite nations and, with other things, caused Israel to be dispersed among the nations. But Baal worship lives on and the spirit continues to strangle individuals, families, and nations.

Baal is the strongman behind sexual perversion and financial greed (fertility practices leading to a crop increase, which is actually materialistic greed). Those who open themselves up to this spirit soon discover how quickly they are overcome. If they align themselves with this spirit on an ongoing basis, they will find it difficult to break free and cannot do so on their own. The nature of deception is such that the deceived one does not know how entrapped he or she becomes until it is too late.

Baal always goes after the next generation, trying to cut off the extension of God's covenantal purposes. He is a violent spirit and even requires human sacrifice. Abortion is under Baal's influence as the appetite for flesh can only be satisfied by death. Just as "cutting" has become popular among today's younger generation, Baal worshipers also engaged in the practice (see 1 Kings 18:28). The prophets of Baal in Canaanite times cut themselves and danced around the fire before Elijah. Baal is fighting hard to avert the great awakening planned for the next generation by enslaving many in pornography and fantasy. It is also subverting today's men and women from stepping into their destinies and the fullness of the anointing.

Baal is the principality over the world and his influence must be broken in men and women who are called to carry the anointing. Once the stronghold is released, I believe, people will move in a freedom of the Holy Spirit as never before and churches will see such an increase in the abiding presence of the Lord rather than a situational or subtle sense of His presence. Baal's influence extends beyond the sexual; it is also seen in the increase of occult activity around the world. It is rooted in occult worship focused on ancient fertility rites. And it feels welcome to reside and nest in places where sexual expression is given free reign. Consider this: those in the Church who are giving their time, money, and focus to Baal through Internet pornography are probably not giving their time, money, and focus to the Lord. The Church is very much impacted. Not only spiritually. As those spirits trail in the doors and affect the atmosphere, those they influence also are limited financially.

Leanne Payne, author of *The Healing Presence*, is well known as an anointed prophet who focused her ministry on helping men in ministry break free from sexual issues, including pornography and homosexuality, that undermine their anointing. During her Pastoral Care Ministry Schools,[5] she addresses the topic of Baal's influence on our culture and how to break its hold. She writes:

> The people of Yahweh always had to withstand a people under the influence of Baal. Or they were overcome by Baal and under his influence. Elijah's task was to bring them out from under the demonic stronghold.[6]

I attended a Leanne Payne conference once at the request of a man I had been dating and was very much in love with. He told me that he was struggling with homosexuality, and I was shocked. I never suspected that anyone as masculine as he was would have thoughts in that direction. I went to try to understand more about sexual issues that men struggled with and to see if there was any hope for us to experience a normal marriage. In the process, I received more healing than I ever thought I needed.

Leanne's ministry followed a pattern of teaching and ministry that was designed to build on one another and lead people right into the healing they needed. She taught about self-hatred, guilt, and shame and helped people break the cycle. She talked about true masculinity and true femininity and what that was according to God's plan. At one point, she asked the whole room to stand and renounce Baal and Asherah worship and led us in a prayer of repentance. The prayer seems liturgical, more of a statement than words anointed with the presence of God. We all recited the scripted prayer after her. Suddenly, the room became electric and alive as several people fell or convulsed on the floor, the sexual deviancy broken as Baal screamed his way out the door. I saw more deliverance occur within just a couple of minutes than I had ever seen before. Homosexuals, those caught in pornography, men and women who had been raped and abused—all seemed to experience an instant deliverance.

Undeniably, once people had received a measure of counsel and teaching, if they were still not able to walk a "straight" walk, they needed a little deliverance. And Baal was the one who had to go.

How many men have lost their anointing, quenched the Spirit, and forfeited their inheritance for another hour of porn? Or a side trip to a prostitute? Leanne Payne would say that what they have abdicated is not just their anointing, but their true masculinity. How many women have lost their true femininity due to the cultural influence of Baal?

In *The Healing Presence*, Leanne talks about Gideon in Judges 6:25-26, who was called to tear down the altars to Baal and lead Israel out. She referred to him as one who came into his true masculinity and led Israel out of their sexual sin and compulsions. That same calling that was upon Gideon is part of the calling of a prophet or minister even today.

We now see this happen in large groups where hundreds are set free. But it is not something a Christian leader would begin to do before God has fully prepared him to minister in such a way. It is part of a prophetic ministry, one that has first of all called the people to a radical repentance, and is thereby enabled to minister deeply to the essential spirit and soul of the people. The prophets are indeed the healers...and that is because their call to repentance is clarion-clear. There is no uncertain sound in their message.... The minister who has, to any extent, reconciled good and evil can never call others to repentance for the trumpet he blows will give a very uncertain sound. A clarion call like that of the Baptist's or Christ's is required.[7]

The most solid men and women I have ever met are those who walk so closely in tune with the Holy Spirit that they begin to radiate His presence, which is the true anointing. They know that the anointing is something that needs to be protected and cherished. They walk in pure love and unadulterated power.

## All That Glitters Is Not Gold

When we think of moral failure, most of us immediately jump to the conclusion that the immoral behavior is linked to sex. That definition of moral failure is extending into the arena of ethical failure as we hear about the supernaturalists manufacturing signs and wonders, and individuals fabricating their testimonies. Their reasons may include an effort to validate or expand their ministry reputations, or to draw more attention to the supernaturalness of their lives. Gold dust is shaken out of hair, oil gushes out of podiums and along doorposts, manna from Heaven that once vanished overnight (like it did in the desert) now lingers longer, and gemstones are bought by the baggie online and kicked out of shoes or secretly tossed when no one is looking. The list of names of those who have been found to perpetuate this fraud is growing longer. Some, you can find on the Internet. Others are just acting immaturely and do not need to be named. God is giving them every opportunity to stop before He exposes the fact that all that glitters is not gold.

Authentic manifestations of gold dust and gemstones and oil do appear...as genuine signs that make you wonder. Unfortunately, the fraudulent manufacturing of such things rob us from the joy of receiving the true manifestations that are genuinely God. So, we cannot jump to conclusions and say every gemstone is a fake expression when some may really, truly be God. I want to celebrate what God is doing and the wonderful bridal adornment heralding the return of the King—as some interpret the symbolic meaning behind the gemstone phenomena. I want to be childlike in my faith and hope and believe all things are from God. But my brothers and sisters are muddying the waters of worship by falsifying signs and wonders. And I have come to see that all that glitters is not gold…and all that sparkles is not a real diamond.

I had one pastor tell me that a young man, who showed great promise and moved in great power, was recently discovered to have fabricated many of the signs and wonders, including gemstones and gold dust appearing. He wasn't sure what to do with him or how to work out the matter within his church.

Another pastor routinely invited a couple to come and minister. The hallmark of their ministry was the sign that followed their teaching— the sign was that people would find gemstones on the ground or in odd locations where he spoke. After talking with the husband about his teaching and how he interpreted the phenomenon of gemstones falling during their meetings, I was quite taken by his sincerity and the love he had for Jesus and others. He seemed very genuine. But I was incredulous to discover that he was kicking gemstones out of his shoes and tossing them into dark corners of the room when no one was looking. I saw him in action and my pastor friends refused to believe me when I explained how he did it. He was later exposed as a fraud and admitted to "seeding the atmosphere with gemstones" so that the angels would begin to do it as well. My friends were too embarrassed to tell me that he had been exposed. I read about it on the Internet months after it came to light.

Why do such sincere people perpetuate fraud? Most are ambitious to build a great ministry reputation and expand their opportunities for itinerant ministry as well. Who do you believe anymore? And how to you treat them? My pastor friends invited him back to minister after he repented. In subsequent meetings, gemstones still fell as a sign and a wonder "validating" his anointing and authority.

How you approach and confront young, up-and-coming revival-ists is very different from confronting someone who has developed an international reputation, or who encourages the fabrication of signs and wonders in his church because it benefits him in some way. The young should respond to the pastors and leaders who are raising them up. Older ones may need a more subtle and honoring approach. I let one minister know that the signs and wonders that he displayed during a meeting I had attended were later tested. Nothing more was said. Since that day, his ministry stopped manifesting those signs. Why? I believe he repented. His true anointing was so great that he did not need to manufacture a fraudulent sign to draw further attention to himself. The pressures to compete for attention and finances are huge—especially in this economy. No one is beyond temptation, but everyone is within reach of grace.

## We Are in a Season of Grace

If you have fallen into some form of sexual sin or fraud, you need to know that we are all walking in a season of grace that began with Christ's death and resurrection and continues until He comes again. It is not too late for you to step into your anointing.

It is one thing to feel godly sorrow well up in your heart for the ones you have hurt, quite another to come to the point of realizing the spiritual implications of mucking around within the Holy of Holies. All are invited to minister—but only some are invited to come closer to the Lord. They may enter the Holy of Holies due to their integrity. Their closeness to God releases an increase in authority and power.

*The Levites who went far from Me when Israel went astray and who wandered from Me after their idols must bear the consequences of their sin. They may serve in My sanctuary, having charge of the gates of the temple and serving in it; they may slaughter the burnt offerings and sacrifices for the people and stand before the people and serve them. But because they served them in the presence of their idols and made the house of Israel fall into sin, therefore I have sworn with uplifted hand that they must bear the consequences of their sin, declares the Sovereign Lord. They are not to come near to serve Me as priests or come near any of My holy things or My most holy offerings; they must bear the shame of their detestable practices. Yet I will put them in charge of the duties of the temple and all the work that is to be done in it.*

*But the priests, who are Levites and descendants of Zadok and who faithfully carried out the duties of My sanctuary when the Israelites went astray from Me, are to come near to minister before Me; they are to stand before Me to offer sacrifices of fat and blood, declares the Sovereign Lord. They alone are to enter My sanctuary; they alone are to come near My table to minister before Me and perform My service* (Ezekiel 44:10-16).

How close do you want to come to Jesus? It is not too late. The Old Testament ways have given way to a new season of grace. Jesus' atonement on the cross ushered in a season of grace that will last until He comes again. Hebrews 9:11-15 speaks to this:

*When Christ came as high priest of the good things that are already here, He went through the greater and more perfect tabernacle that is not man-made, that is to say, not a part of this creation. He did not enter by means of the blood of goats and calves; but He entered the Most Holy Place once for all by His own blood, having obtained eternal redemption. The blood of goats and bulls and the ashes of a heifer sprinkled on those who are ceremonially unclean sanctify them so that they are outwardly clean. How much more, then, will the blood of Christ, who through the eternal Spirit offered Himself unblemished to God, cleanse our consciences from acts that lead to death, so that we may serve the living God!*

*For this reason Christ is the mediator of a new covenant, that those who are called may receive the promised eternal inheritance—now that He has died as a ransom to set them free from the sins committed under the first covenant.*

When Christ comes again, He will bring the fullness of salvation to those who believe in Him.

*It was necessary, then, for the copies of the heavenly things to be purified with these sacrifices, but the heavenly things themselves with better sacrifices than these. For Christ did not enter a man-made sanctuary that was only a copy of the true one; He entered heaven itself, now to appear for us in God's presence. Nor did He enter heaven to offer Himself again and again, the way the high priest enters the Most Holy Place every year with blood that is not his own. Then Christ would have had to suffer many times since the creation of the world. But now He has appeared once for all at the end of the ages to do away with sin by the sacrifice of Himself. Just as man is destined to die once, and after that to face judgment, so Christ was sacrificed once to take away the sins of many people; and He will appear a second time, not to bear sin, but to bring salvation to those who are waiting for Him (Hebrews 9:23-28).*

During this season of grace—the time between the New Covenant and Christ's second coming—anything is possible, but it is up to you to respond to God's grace. Most of us came in out of the shadows of the world steeped in the sinful ways of the world. God's embrace washed us of our sin, and our hearts leapt at the sight and sound and sense of His presence. Some have fallen asleep again, or turned back to the ways of the world. Others have gone off the deep end of the pool and are drowning. If you have walked away from relationship with Jesus, if you have tossed your crown by the wayside, and trampled on the anointing, you need to know this—you are still living in the season of grace. You can come back and begin to restore all that the enemy has stolen, but you cannot restore the time that you have lost. Why waste more time?

We are living in a season of grace. Where sin abounds, grace all the more abounds. Grace has a face. It is Jesus. Grace has a way of dealing with offensive behaviors—it is called love. When I was a child and a young teen, grieving my parents the most, I remember my father wrapping me in his embrace and saying, "I love you." His love shattered my rebellion. It is no different with Jesus. His love shatters our rebellion. How is His love expressed? Through us—to one another.

When we read the hurts of others who felt not the love and grace extended, but the judgment and anger expressed, it is an opportunity for us to learn how to love better. Restoration is a two-way street. It is about helping another to heal—along with those whom he or she has hurt. It is also about the Church learning how to love one another—and extending grace. There are those who move away and cannot receive the process of restoration or desire to remain in fellowship. So we let them go—but we must let them know that the door is always open so long as we all live in this season of grace that began on the cross and extends until the second coming of Christ.

If you want an exponential increase of power in your life, cultivate the grace that sets you free and come into the fullness of your restoration and salvation.

The anointing raised to the third power depends on you walking not only in dunamis, but also with a soundness of mind and integrity that cannot be shaken.

## Endnotes

1. J. Lee Grady, "Holding Paul Cain's Feet to the Fire," *Charisma Online,* 2006, www.fireinmybones.com/Columns/040406. html (accessed November 30, 2011).

2. Telephone interview with author and John Paul Jackson.

3. John Paul Jackson, "Restoring Fallen Leaders," http://ngca.org/custom_files/restoring.htm (accessed November 30, 2011).

4. Telephone interview with author and Barbara Yoder.

5. Pastoral Care Ministry Schools, www.leannepayne.org/home/index.php.

6. Leanne Payne, *The Healing Presence: Curing the Soul through Union with Christ* (Grand Rapids: Baker, 1995), 234.

7. *ibid.*, 238-239.

# LET THE ANOINTING FLOW

**Julia:**

Lord, what would You have us know about the future of the anointing?

**Jesus:**

*The world craves strong leadership. It always has and always will seek leaders to guide them in times of war and uncertainty. Those who are full of My wisdom, who inquire of the Lord when facing decisions, step into the mind of Christ—the vast reservoir of knowledge set apart for the nations that wisdom created before the worlds were made, can be accessed through prayer and received through revelation.*

*These leaders know that in their weakness, I am strong. Their weakness leads them to Me. My strength and empowerment sends them out. My leaders are being called out. And many are listening. They know that they have been born for purpose. Their sacred destiny is about to unfold.*

*Many are like Gideon, threshing wheat in a winepress that hides them from sight. Focusing on their daily bread rather than the wine of My blood and My blood-bought Bride, they are afraid of the spirit of this age that was worshiped and established by their fathers. Trying valiantly not to bow down to the Baals, they are secretly developing the heart of a warrior. I am releasing an anointing to break them out of hiding, empower their confidence in Me, and transform them into warriors full of strategy that will propel them into national significance overnight. Every family, every community, every corporation, and every nation will have its Gideon. The Lord is with you, mighty warrior! (See Judges 6:12.) Go in the strength you have…am I not sending you? (See Judges 6:14.)*

*Gideons arise! Your hour has come!*

*Elijahs are appointing Elishas who are anointing Jehus who will ride out against the spirit of this age and release justice in the darkest of places, because they know there can be no peace in places where idolatry and witchcraft abound (See 2 Kings 9:22). The anointing of power to undo the works of the enemy—discernment and strategies for spiritual warfare—is coming upon you. I anoint you.*

*Jehus arise! This is the time for your warrior anointing to step up!*

*Deborahs are stepping into political arenas with divine strategies that will result in peace. Esthers have broken through with prayer that releases young women around the world to step into their sacred destinies. There is no limit* to what a heart so full of love can do. "The nations will see your righteousness, and all kings your glory; you will be called by a new name that the mouth of the Lord will bestow" (Isa. 62:2).

*Deborahs arise! The nations are calling you!*

Leaders of Israel, First Nations people, every tribe and tongue, every nation's redemptive gifts and revelatory anointing are being revealed in this hour. For you are the revelation of Christ; the message of eternity flows through you. My anointing flows through the one and through the corporate body of every people group. Isolated, you are weak. Gathered together, My Spirit flows more freely. "Your sun will never set again, and your moon will wane no more; the Lord will be your everlasting light, and your days of sorrow will end. Then will all your people be righteous and they will possess the land forever...." (Isa. 60:20-21).

*Come forth you tribal peoples! Speak the eternal sacred destiny!*

The future of your anointing is this—walk with Me, intentionally, prayerfully, draw aside to be with Me, and I will calm the storms within you and then through you. Arise, shine, for your light has come, and the glory of the Lord rises upon you. See, thick darkness covers the earth and thick darkness is over the people, but the Lord rises upon you and His glory appears over you. Nations will come to your light, and kings to the brightness of your dawn. (See Isaiah 60:1-3.)

*Come. I am calling you.*

Chapter Seven

# RELEASING THE ANOINTING IN EVERYDAY LIFE

Releasing God's presence is His will for you and your inheritance on earth. We are living in a season of grace where more of the anointing is available and, if we are wise, we will keep our lamps full of that oil as well as give it away. No matter what your view is of the endtimes, whether your theology supports the elect being raptured before, during, or after a tribulation, or even if you believe it is all symbolic, one thing is clear—this earth is our inheritance and our responsibility to steward. The Kingdom of God is also our inheritance and our responsibility to steward. Whether that Kingdom is a place being prepared for us or a reality that we are living out, Christ in us is the hope of glory, for us and through us.

If you have awakened to the Anointed One, you know what I am talking about. We have seasons of grace where we live in that hope of glory and other seasons of grace where we release that hope of glory to others. The glory and the anointing is the essence of His presence, alive and tangible. It is so present and yet so elusive that it takes an encounter with God to open the eyes of our hearts and show us how close that glory is. It takes an encounter to reveal how thin the barrier is between the natural and the supernatural—and what we are called to do with it.

There is a progression of anointing available to us all. It begins with us awakening to the Anointed One and releasing that ability to awaken others to Jesus. We start to walk in the normal Christian life—full of the Holy Spirit and power. And as we walk into our destiny as Ambassadors of Christ in our local churches and communities, it becomes evident that many are called to increasing spheres of influence, and many enter into the governmental aspects of ministry often referred to as the fivefold ministries of apostles, prophets, pastors, evangelists, and teachers.

## Launching the Awakening Through Prayer

Jeannie Fuller and Karen Berner are two women who are fully awakened to the love of God. Their anointing in intercession is powerful and hidden. They focus on the face of God and listen for His heartbeat, and then they release what they see and hear in prayer.

Often, the ministry of prayer is not all that popular in your average church. Places like International House of Prayer in Kansas City have spawned other houses of prayer around the world where 24-hour prayer and worship infuse communities with the ever-increasing presence of God.

Prayer is the basis of communication with God: our dialog begins there, intimacy grows as we hear His heart beating through ours, and our lives change the more we spend time in the presence of the Holy Spirit. Prayer changes lives, launches revivals, and rivets the attention of God toward us. Prayer, although the fruit of it remains largely unseen for a time, is very powerful.

Jeannie and Karen's intercession took an interesting turn one day when they realized that God was calling them beyond intercessory prayer. It was time for intercessory action, and that realization caused them to trust God to provide for a three-year journey to complete a mission to pray in every state of the United States.[1] Jeannie and Karen have both shared stories from their journey with me through the past couple of years. The fact that they actually paid a price to obey God and go where He sent them to do a task that would have no visible fruit astounds me in this day and age when we want to see the results of any funds we invest in an endeavor. But the Kingdom of God is not like our earthly, results-oriented kingdom of this world. Intercession is a hidden work of inestimable value.

Jeannie talked about the beginning of their journey into the heart of God for America:

> Our journey began in 2008. While I was in prayer, I heard the Lord say, "Ring the Liberty Bell over the nation and proclaim freedom." So I took it into intercession. I didn't think I was actually going to go on an intercessory prayer journey around the country. Several weeks after my encounter in prayer, I saw online a Chuck Pierce word that seemed to confirm what I was hearing. His word said, "Hear the bells this week! There's a sound of liberty coming from Heaven. There's a sound I'm bringing in. Every time you hear those bells of change, decree a new liberty is coming before you, and coming upon you, and that you will enter the fields of freedom."
>
> Then, my friend Karen Berner and I, right before the November presidential elections, went to pray in Kansas City. While driving down the road we saw a Liberty Bell sign and I

thought that was no coincidence. So, I told Karen what the Lord had been speaking to me about the Liberty Bell and we prayed about it. That week, we received an invitation to pray in Louisiana. Just before we left, I decided to see if there was a Liberty Bell in that state. Online, I saw that every state has a replica of the Liberty Bell—usually at the state capital.

On the Liberty Bell itself is the inscription of Leviticus 25:10 [KJV] where the Lord tells the people to declare freedom over all the inhabitants of the earth: *"Proclaim LIBERTY throughout all the land unto all the inhabitants thereof."* The bell represents freedom. Different groups have gone to the Liberty Bell and rang it over history. At one time, after the Civil War, the original Liberty Bell went on tour from state to state to promote unity and freedom. Abolitionists of the civil war, and later the women's suffrage movement, latched onto the Liberty Bell as a proclamation of freedom.

Jeannie and Karen prayed in Louisiana together and rang the Liberty Bell at the state capitol at the end of their time of intercession. By then, Jeannie had realized that God was calling her to actually go to each state and pray in person—not just from the comfort of her own home. Karen wasn't convinced that God was calling her to commit to the journey with Jeannie. During a trip to Israel later that year, Karen brought the matter before the Lord. According to Karen:

> It was such a huge commitment to pray for the whole country that I decided I would stay at the wailing wall in Jerusalem until I had an answer from the Lord about going along.

> He told me clearly that He wanted me to carry His heart throughout the country and pray into God's love for Israel and the Jews everywhere we went. He also said that there would be a revelation for the sake of the Church and the sake of the country, about how America and Israel are intrinsically

tied together. One cannot come into the fullness of destiny without the other. We were to pray into the political and economic destinies and that the values of God's Kingdom would come forth.

Two days later, I wandered into a park in Jerusalem called Liberty Bell Park and saw a replica of the Liberty Bell that had been gifted to Israel by the United States. It was an immediate confirmation of the word the Lord had spoken to me at the wall.

Karen was in! The two women began planning their trip and as funds came available and their families' schedules allowed, they traveled from state to state. Jeannie tells the rest of the story:

God showed us that we were to pray for the captives to be set free. We used Isaiah 61 as the basis of what we were to decree and prophesy over the nation. We declared that the captives would be set free and that the people in the land would start receiving Him. One of the things we prayed was that the man-made idols that keep people in bondage would come down. We've seen news reports that those structures are being broken down and people are coming back to Him in a really personal way after we prayed in specific states.

The journey was a really transforming experience. I had prayed for the nations but I never saw as clearly how all the people groups around the world are connected and how if one nation is in bondage—especially our nation because we have so much influence—the other nations come into bondage. He taught us about liberty and authority. He opened doors for us to access the bells in some states and go into the senate and house chambers and pray. The most special ones were the ones that didn't have limited access. The ones where we could totally ring the bell, the sound that went out was most impacting.

We wondered what to do if we could not ring the bell because it was locked or inaccessible, or didn't have a ringer. So, we brought our own bell. Karen had one of her mother-in-law's bells that dated back 100 years old. In early days they used to use the bell to awaken the town, to issue the call to meetings or fire and emergencies. It made sense to me that the bell would represent an awakening. So we prayed for revival in each state and to awaken the angels to move throughout the state and release the ministry God wanted to impart. We would ring those bells to wake the angels up in the area and to seal the decree of freedom. In some places, we used our own makeshift ringer.

The stories from each state are really powerful and full of divine appointments with people. In Colorado, I was getting ready to ring the Liberty Bell that was located out in the courtyard of the capitol when this bus pulled up filled with children. They saw us and ran over to ask what we were doing. We explained that we were ringing the bell for freedom. It didn't have a ringer but we had drumsticks to use and handed them to the kids who yelled FREEDOM! as they struck it.

Because so much of our journey involved driving—like one seven-day drive taking us to 11 states—we really got to see the country and get a glimpse of God's heart. Driving through these small towns made me realize how much God loves America. He absolutely loves this place and the people in this nation. When you are in prayer, you feel the Father's heart and He releases prayers through you and you cannot help but fall in love with what He loves.

## The Normal Christian Life

I believe in the power of prayer to transform lives and cities and nations. I also believe that intercessory prayer should result in intercessory action. God may call you to a prayer journey, or to reach out and minister to others in your daily life. Moving in response to His invitation, obeying His call, and releasing His authority, love, and power is the normal Christian life.

Not long ago, I found myself speaking to a group of Presbyterian women who had asked me to come and mentor them during a weekend leadership retreat. Every one of them was full of excitement about what God was doing in their women's group and in their church. They were running a Holy Spirit Boot Camp at the church and people were getting saved, healed, and delivered. The men's ministry leaders took note and wanted what they had. The pastor kept sneaking into the women's meetings ready to receive all that God had for him, too. These women were stepping out in their prophetic and teaching gifts and thought the supernatural was super fun.

Throughout the weekend, they used the word *supernatural* a lot. Their constant use of the word bothered me until I figured out why. One morning I told them that their language might be a barrier to some who are unsure about bringing the Holy Spirit's presence and power into an evangelical, traditional setting. I challenged them to see the work of Christ not as supernatural, but as modeling the normal Christian life. The supernatural was meant to become super-normal in our day and age. Healing the sick, releasing prophecies, setting the captives free, ministering healing in all its forms, loving others into their sacred destinies—all are expressions of the normal Christian life. Using the word *supernatural* made people feel uncomfortable, or created a sense that they were into spiritualism or the occult, or indicated that they should all get into some aspect of woo-woo faith. Start using the phrase: "The normal Christian life includes all that Christ modeled," and you raise the bar of belief and intercessory action.

Jesus' disciples woke up to who Jesus is. They got excited when Jesus started modeling His extraordinary abilities to read people's hearts and minds and to touch them and physically heal individuals to such a degree that crowds took notice and communities were transformed. In the early days of Jesus' earthly ministry, Jesus preached good news to the poor, elevating their status in society. He demonstrated miracles and gave us the Sermon on the Mount, establishing what the normal Christian life should look like and hinting at the power to come that is available to all (see Matt. 5-7).

## Redemptive "Waste"

We are all marginal people from obscure places—fishermen, tax collectors, children, women, and people from nations despised by other nations—just like the early believers in the Gospels. And just like them, we are called to a sacred destiny that lifts us out of the ordinary world and into the extraordinary where housewives become backdoor prophets, retirees extend God's healing power throughout their communities, loggers become evangelists, and small groups become powerhouses where the presence of God resides and transforms individuals. We begin where we are and step out according to our faith.

Don is one of my neighbors here on an island in the Pacific Northwest, and he attends a local Foursquare Church. One day, he was walking along the shore of the island when he saw a couple with their five children gathering driftwood. As the father passed by, Don asked him what they were gathering driftwood for. The man replied, "We burn it in our woodstove. We can't afford the heating bill in the winter so this is what we do."

Don knew that burning salt-laden wood quickly corrodes the woodstove and chimney and that driftwood should not be burned. The fire hazard outweighed the savings. Another thought came to mind as well: *If this family was in need of wood, how many others were doing the same thing, scrounging the beach so they could stay warm in the Northwestern damp and rainy winters?*

His eyes were opened that day to a need that he felt prompted to fill. Don started gathering firewood and, as others heard what he was doing, people began donating firewood for him to distribute to single mothers, widows, and families in need. Initially, Don had piles of firewood in his front yard that he would load into a pickup he purchased for the ministry. Then he would drive it out to the homes on his list, unload it, and repeat, usually by himself. It took him two weeks to deliver the initial loads to the people on his list.

Wood donations poured in with a mixture of split logs and kindling from lumberyards and logging operations. On occasion, people donated trees from their property, and Don and a few men from the church would go out and split and load the logs. Eventually, a local lumberyard offered the use of a forklift and truck. The wood was tossed into bins made up of pallets and loaded onto the truck by a forklift. Truck, driver, forklift, and Don made the rounds in record time.

The wood deliveries led to greater spiritual influence in the community than Don ever anticipated. Don found himself talking to the men who rode with him and helped in the ministry. He realized that he was mentoring them as a father would a son, listening to their hurts and family concerns and ministering wisdom, truth, and the love of the Father, one-on-one. It was a time to be cherished, a bonding time between spiritual father and son.

Once they unloaded the wood, Don would ask if they could pray for the recipient. Almost everyone says yes. Their hearts melted as Don's fatherly prayer and natural provision of wood strangely warmed their hearts. Many of these people have never, nor would ever, walk into a church; but they are awakening to the love of God right at home. Don brings something of the normal Christian life to them...without the pressure to conform to a specific religion or belief. He brings the love and power to change hearts of believers and unbelievers alike and lifts people out of the bondage of wintertime debt. Don is walking in the normal Christian life—receiving God's love and giving it away.

Don took what was considered waste—scrap wood or fallen trees—and saw that it could meet a need in his community. But Don moved out into ministry because he knew that whatever he did for the least of these, he was doing unto the Lord (see Matt. 25:45).

Watchman Nee, writing in The Normal Christian Life, believes that this is where we start—not by using our gifts and anointing to create a spectacular ministry, but to step out and minister to the Lord, wasting our lives on Him.

> But we have to remember this, that He will never be satisfied without our 'wasting' ourselves upon Him. Have you ever given too much to the Lord? May I tell you something? One lesson some of us have come to learn is this; that in Divine service the principle of waste is the principle of power. The principle, which determines usefulness, is the very principle of scattering. Real usefulness in the hand of God is measured in terms of 'waste.' The more you think you can do, and the more you employ your gifts up to the very limit (and some even go over the limit!) in order to do it, the more you find that you are applying the principle of the world and not of the Lord. God's ways with us are all designed to establish in us this other principle, namely, that our work *for* Him springs out of our ministering *to* Him. I do not mean that we are going to do nothing; but the first thing for us must be the Lord Himself, not His work.[2]

## Seeking and Saving the Lost

Evie was my spiritual mentor during my early 20s. A large swarthy woman with bobbed, jet black hair, she definitely carried God's authority and presence with her wherever she went. Everyone took notice of her, consciously or unconsciously, when she entered a room. I wandered into the church she attended like a lost and broken waif, grieving the death of my fiancé and deeply depressed about life. Her disarming smile and loving, "Hi Honey!" immediately made me comfortable. Somehow, she saw both the grief I carried and the potential destiny of my life at the same moment and knew that one was about to cancel the other—which one, only time would tell. She reached out to minister to me, taking me in as if I were one of her own children. At first, I thought she was a mere housewife. I was soon to recognize that she was one of God's backdoor prophets, a stealth healer, and a subtle evangelist to hundreds who have been touched by her ministry. She is one who has always risen to the task of seeking and saving the lost, boldly taking the mission of Jesus into her everyday life.

A woman given to prayer and intercession, Evie seemed to have a direct hotline to God. If God spoke to her about someone in distress, Evie would go to that person. And if the person didn't answer her phone or the door, God would direct Evie to the place where the person could be found.

Once, Evie received a distress call from a woman who knew her reputation as God's social worker. Apparently, the woman's ex-husband was on his way over and she felt frightened enough to call for backup. Evie pulled into the woman's driveway at the same time the man arrived. Angry and belligerent, the man acted like a wild animal out of control as he ranted and raved about his wife and life. God had already armed Evie with two words of knowledge on her drive over. Acting on the first one, Evie asked the man if he was taking antidepressants. The man admitted that he was on Prozac®. "Did you know," said Evie, "that Prozac® builds up in your system and in a man, that buildup can make you more hostile than you really are? And that Prozac® can make a man homicidal?"

His eyes grew wide with surprise as Evie continued to draw him into reality, letting the man know that his anger was not the real him.

His agitation subsided as he heard her continue speaking, her voice calming him. Finally, he broke down weeping, apologizing for his anger, and asking for help.

"Why don't you give me the keys to the car and the trunk and go on inside the house; OK?" Evie said with supernatural authority that the man responded to. He handed over the keys and asked if she knew what was in there. She said God told her his trunk contained several guns and he was there to kill his wife. He nodded, his head drooping in shame and repentance.

She told him that she was going to call 911 and tell them that he was having a reaction to antidepressants and that he was OK for now. He nodded again and went into the house peacefully while Evie remained outside by the car. The police arrived and took custody of the man and the guns they found in his trunk.

Evie has intervened in the lives of many throughout her decades as a backdoor prophet and led hundreds of people to the Lord. Along the way, lives were saved and transformed. Young women realized that abortion was not the best decision they could make. Other women realized that they could leave a life-threatening marriage, and many stepped into their gifts and calling as Evie spoke words of destiny to them. The authority that backed her words seemed supernatural to most of us. Intimidating to many, in fact. But her secret history of relationship with God enabled her to move in obedience. Because she acted so often on the prompting of the Holy Spirit, she walked in the assurance that what God had called her to do, He would back up. She walked in the fullness of her authority and in power. As a result, she knew that the safest place to be is in God's perfect will—every day.

## Shifting the Shadows of Darkness

You are the light of the world—so Jesus says about not only Himself but also you. No matter where you go, that light in you shines through the fallen atmosphere of this world and shifts the shadows of darkness far away. The presence of God in you is greater than the darkness that seems so prevalent in the hearts and minds of those you come in contact with during your everyday routine of life. On your worst days, your light still shines. On your best days, you may even go out and intentionally release the presence of God in your everyday life. Living with the mindset that God has called you to release His presence more intentionally will enable you to see the shadows shift and your light shine in such a way that you discover that the gifts of the Spirit have become integrated with your personality. Revealing the goodness and love and power of God becomes a part of your day, every day.

Clashing with the demonic influences in our culture seems to happen when we least expect it. Not long ago, I visited my cousin and her family in Massachusetts just in time to attend a Saturday barbecue hosted by her old friends who happened to be a gay couple. It was summertime so we sat outside in the warm afternoon breeze eating and drinking, socializing with both straight and gay couples. I noticed a man making the rounds of the tables, asking a few questions and either being invited to sit down or moving away. Eventually, we locked eyes. This aging, gay man with huge, milky-blue eyes sat down at the table where I was eating with my cousin and her husband, both whom are not believers. The man said he wanted to read my Tarot cards and proceeded to pull out the deck of cards.

Much to my surprise, I replied that he should let me read his cards instead. I've never read Tarot cards, nor did I understand what they were all about. I simply knew that it was an occult counterfeit of the revelatory gifts. I decided to show him the real gift in action and trusted that Jesus would give me a prophetic word for him as I played with the deck.

He recoiled and said, "NO!" So I asked why not and he said, "I don't trust you!"

"But you approach strangers to read their cards. Why not let me read yours?" I persisted.

After a long, cold stare, he begrudgingly cut the deck and slapped a card upright on top. I gazed at it and prayed for God's word and heart to come alive to this man, then proceeded to give him a prophetic word. I spoke about where he had been, the first major betrayal and hurt in his life, where he had gone from there, and what his destiny could still be like. He listened intently, his face softening as he realized that love, not death, sought to touch his heart. He recognized a different spirit at work and said he really liked the word. We talked for a short while about the word, and he confirmed its accuracy in the presence of my cousin who was quite astonished by the display of God's authentic prophetic gift.

As the conversation drew to a close, I started praying for the man silently. Suddenly, his face started twitching and he started stammering his words as the spirit at work in him began to manifest. He hastily gathered up his cards and little crystal ball, stuffing them into a drawstring bag as he prepared to leave my table and make his getaway...but not without realizing that the Holy Spirit is the *Great Power* and that God really does know all about his life and loves him anyway.

Jesus never shied away from those who were demonized or involved in the occult. He met them right where they stood or partied and revealed the Kingdom of God. Sadly, not everyone responds favorably to a God-encounter. The man at the party was not ready to renounce his occult involvement. Many who are demonized are so under the influence of the demonic that they cannot make a personal choice about whether to receive Christ and deliverance or not. For some, it takes repeat encounters as if they want to see who's got the greatest power.

While working in Europe, I spent an evening having dinner with a few colleagues. The discussion turned away from work and into the arena of faith as I shared about the *Shifting Shadows* book series that was in the early stages of development. We talked about the varieties of spiritual experiences, from what we call "intuition" to the differences between God's power and the occult counterfeit.

One woman, who was from the town I was living in at the time, seemed to be living in that parallel universe of occult counterfeit. As she talked, it became evident that her spiritual experiences were similar to what I had experienced. She was so intrigued by the stories I told her of a recent trip to Brazil where I saw miracles of nature and healing occur, that she talked openly about her recent encounters.

"You know, I went to Brazil to see a psychic healer named John of God not too long ago. Have you heard of him?" she asked.

"Yeah! I just happened to be in a town located close to John of God's compound. I was traveling with a healing evangelist and saw hundreds of people getting healed and delivered, receiving visions, and encountering God in wonderful ways," I said, realizing that we were on a parallel journey.

John of God is a psychic healer and a medium who channels over 30 spirit entities—spirits that treat ailments such as cancer, AIDS, blindness, asthma, drug addiction, alcohol abuse, tumors, etc. Every year, hundreds of people journey to his compound located in a small town in the middle of Brazil. His "work" was featured on an Oprah Winfry show in 2010. His spectacular methods were on camera for all to watch as he scraped people's eyeballs or rammed a rod up their nasal cavity or performed surgery, without anesthesia and often with a rusty knife. Some claimed they were healed. Others later died of their preexisting conditions. As people waited in his waiting room and spent a few hours in meditation, they often reported that the hours passed like minutes before they were called in for their healing consultation. Clearly, they had come into a zone where the spirits began their demonic work.

"Not only that, but I went with another group in Brazil to see a faith healer," she added. "We all took this herb, this drug, before the meeting started and what happened was so amazing. We all saw the same vision at the same time and people started getting spontaneously healed. It sounds just like what you experienced," she said in reference to another story I had told about a miracle of nature (see *Shifting Shadows of Supernatural Power* for the complete story).

"No, similar but different. We weren't taking drugs. We could all see what was happening to others. We all witnessed the same nature miracle with the untimely rainstorm I mentioned. But it was not the mass hallucination of a drug-induced experience. It was a reality-based spiritual experience."

Although she was in her early 40s, she was not healthy. As a result, she sought healing in the very system that gave rise to her illnesses. There was no time to set her straight. The conversation was getting a little too wild for the others, so we shifted to safer topics related to our work. But by the end of the dinner, one thing had become startlingly clear to all of us: Spiritual experiences are like shifting shadows. We all experience things that lie outside the realm of our ordinary senses. Some are shadows that cross our path that we barely pay any attention to—intuitions, words of knowledge, special knowing-that-you-knows. Some experiences appear so radiant with light that they bring messages from angels, healing, insights that bring us through the dark nights of our souls. Other experiences appear darker, nightmarish even, like another entity has taken over our bodies, drugged us into hallucinations, lured us deeper into the forests of shadows until darkness overcomes us.

Signs and wonders, prophetic revelation, miracles, and healings are taking place all over the world and seem to be increasing in some streams of charismatic Christianity. Their counterfeit emerges in various streams of the occult. Sometimes, they look eerily similar and leave the watcher wondering, "Could this be God?" Part of our mission in the normal Christian life is to release the light of God and revelation of the truth, to shift the shadows of darkness on the world.

I lost track of my colleague for almost a year but one day, I noticed her walk into my church. A friend of hers had invited her to come and listen to a prophet who was in town and speaking that night. I greeted her warmly, curious to know how the evening would impact her. When the prophet gave an altar call and said he was going to lay hands on everyone in the room, she got into line and let him lay hands on her. I watched closely, expecting some manifestation of the demonic. But she seemed unfazed.

She came over to me with a puzzled expression on her face and asked, "What is the difference between a Christian prophet and New Age prophets? This guy sounds just like the New Age prophets I've been around."

I started to explain the difference between sanctifying the gifts of revelation and revelation that comes from Jesus as well as the difference between occult and Christian power. But it was beyond her understanding, and I felt like I was coming across sounding like we Christians have the superior revelation (which we do). She wasn't asking for head knowledge. She was asking for an authentic encounter with the God of Love. So I took a different approach.

"The difference has to do with the cross and the blood of Christ," I began. My hands made the sign of the cross in front of her as I continued, "The dividing line between Christ's pure revelatory power and occult or New Age power is the cross." I noticed her eyes twitching as I spoke. "And the blood of Christ is what purchased us from the power of the evil one." As I said that, her body started shaking violently.

She stammered that she had to get out of there and excused herself. Clearly, she wasn't ready to surrender to the Redeemer's love at that moment. However, she understood, for the first time, that the blood of Christ and the cross of Christ are the difference between the power of Christians and the power of the occult practitioners.

I don't know where she is today, but God knows.

God also knows that we need to shift the shadows of darkness out of the Church if our corporate light is to shine like a beacon that draws others in. Often, when I attend church, I become aware of the demonic influences dampening the atmosphere. Worship feels flat. I may get a headache if I am sitting next to someone who is particularly demonized. Sometimes I have to move. Other times, I pray for the person. We have no idea what people are carrying when they come to church. Addictions of all kinds, especially sexual addictions in all their forms, like pornography, are rooted in the demonic and Christians are not immune to the influences of the spirit of Baal in our culture. The gift of discernment and opportunities for cleansing and deliverance need to become part of the service if we are going to enter into a corporate anointing and create a place where the Holy Spirit loves to dwell.

One day several years ago, I found myself having lunch with the late Jill Austin, a woman with a creative prophetic ministry, just before she was to minister at an Encounter's Network conference hosted by James Goll. I told her the story about my colleague's confusion about the difference between Christian and New Age prophets and her reaction to the cross and the blood. Then I asked Jill why we didn't seem to focus on the cross in our meetings anymore and wondered aloud what would happen if we did? Jill took it in and didn't reply to my question but as she wrote down my questions in her notepad, I thought she might work it into her meeting. Sure enough, at the end of the meeting, Jill spoke about the cross and the blood and asked everyone to turn and pray for one another to be delivered. As she asked these Christians to release one another from the shifting shadows that played against their anointing, all heaven broke loose. I stood up on a chair off to the side to get a look at the action. Hundreds of people were weeping or manifesting the presence of a demonic spirit that quickly left as they prayed one for another. Jill prayed over the group to hasten the deliverance. Her session broke open the atmosphere for God to move in great healing during the remainder of the conference.

If we are to release the presence of God in everyday life, we need to maintain our focus on the cross and the blood of Christ. It is the cross that defines us and separates us out of the world and unto Jesus. It is the blood that releases the authority and the power we need. Blood-bought believers are the ones carrying the true anointing in the world, an anointing needed to shift the shadows of darkness and release the Kingdom's light.

## Come Closer

There is a price to pay for the anointing. How close do you want to come and how far do you want to go with Jesus? Are you ready to expand your sphere of influence?

James Goll, a prophetic teacher and prolific author who is based in Tennessee,[6] spoke about the anointing and our calling to release God's presence in everyday life during an interview. His insights will guide you in a greater understanding of just how close Jesus is and challenge you to come closer still, reach into Him, and turn and give Him away to others.

The anointing is a supernatural capacity of the Holy Spirit through the life and current day ministry of Jesus Christ, in, upon, and through a believer to impact a person, family, or anything within their sphere of influence because the anointing is more than just about an individual. It comes upon, and then is released through that person. Their measure depends upon their *metron*; that's another Greek word for sphere. So one person's anointing is going to be according to their gift/ call mix, but it is also dependent upon what is their sphere. Some are going to have a true God-gift of healing, but their *metron* of expressing that might not be a crusade. It might be a Starbucks® coffee shop and their assignment is one-on-one.

My definition of the anointing is that it has to be about Jesus. It is the present-day ministry of the Holy Spirit that comes upon, is within, and is released to release a testimony of the goodness of God. If the anointing doesn't leave a fragrance of the goodness of God, I don't think it's a real Christ anointing.

I studied the Scriptures and historical detail about the gate called "Beautiful," knowing that the Holy Spirit was releasing a revelation in our day on what's called the bridal paradigm. In the book of Acts, it was at the gate called Beautiful that Peter came to with some of the disciples. A lame man sat at that gate every day. Everyone would pass him by to go through that gate into the courts of the city. He was well known; probably a professional beggar.

I remember having an experience in a visionary seer realm, where the gate called "Beautiful" came before me and I saw something on the other side of the gate. It was like going from the natural into the eternal, a supernatural dimension. And the veil was so thin, it was permeable. I could see something resting on the other side of this revelation of the beauty realm of God. So I just stretched my hand in and my hand went through the veil of the natural into the eternal. It was like a living substance.

It's hard for me to explain it to you, but this does deal with the anointing. I put my hand in it. I could pick it up and it was lucid. It reflected light and all the colors of the prism of the rainbow also reflected and it glistened. I put my hand in it and felt that living substance. You see the anointing isn't a thing; the anointing is a living substance—it's God Himself. When I reached through it, I saw this whole realm of the beauty of the Lord.

Many prophets have an emphasis on the beauty realm of God and the bridal paradigm. All of that is about the gate that is being opened up by Jesus. When He comes in His triumphant procession, He comes through this gate.

I looked through, and I stretched my hand into this living substance of the tangible, amazing, living anointing. I looked over my shoulder and suddenly I was "living" this encounter in the book of Acts. I saw hurting people on the other side and I was torn because I wanted to go over here and just stay. I just wanted to stay where this living substance was, but there was a challenge given. It deals with the purpose of the anointing. I was to reach my hand in and get it, but I had to look over my shoulder and then bring it out as I saw the lame of today sitting outside the gate called Beautiful. So we've got to learn our way in, into that manifested presence where the tangible reality of the living One resides, because that's the anointing, the *Christos*, the living One. Then we have to pick Him up, carry Him, and turn back around out here in today's world where the people are waiting for a people who have a touch of a supernatural, to meet their needs because they are lame. They can't get through the gate by themselves.

You want to know how I got the anointing I carry? Through a relationship with God; I fasted not because I was told to fast, but because I wanted to fast. I wanted to seek His face. I read His Word not because it was just the right thing to do, but because I wanted to find life. I prayed, not just because it was the fad of the hour that changes the world. All of this is beyond methodology. It's about relational and incarnational Christianity—the Word became flesh and dwelt among us. Now we know that's true about one person, Jesus, who was in the bosom of the Father. He came forth; He took on flesh and dwelt among as a Man. While I say that's true about one, it's actually a model for us all. The Word is to take on flesh and become an embodiment and that doesn't happen just by an equation.

Esther, Hadassah, went through weeks of preparation before she was presented before the King. She had oil treatments—that's the Holy Spirit, and beauty treatments—that's the beauty realm of God. So there was preparation before there was presentation, but there was a cost for the full result.

Now, do we all reach the fullness of our potential? No, but we've got to be faithful according to our sphere or metron, and then your faithfulness brings increase. I think I have been a person who has just been faithful.

One of my keys to the anointing is faithfulness and under-standing the fellowship of His sufferings. I am stuck to Him no matter what. I've been through some hell, but I want to tell you something, my God has never given up on me, and I am here as a covenant man that will never give up on the faithfulness of God. I might not understand everything, but I am going to push the button called "trust in the Lord with all your heart and lean not on your own understanding, in all your ways acknowledge Him and He will direct your path." He will direct your path sometimes, and you'll be blown away by the breadth or depth of the exposure or impact that you have.

## Season of Grace to Increase Your Anointing

If you want to increase in the anointing and release the presence and power of God into everyday life, strengthen your connection and relationship with the Anointed One. Then trust in Him. When you spend time in prayer and worship every morning, you are intention-ally filling your lamp with the oil that burns bright. You go about your daily work and divine appointments happen as people are drawn to the light of His glory. Increase happens simply by spending time in

His presence, or as James Goll says, going through the preparation and beauty treatments.

Recognize that you have a sacred destiny and all power and authority has been given to Jesus. Tap into it to reach your destiny. Seek Him for the grace and means to fulfill your calling in life, for you are living in a place where the fields are ripe for harvest. Your house and your neighborhood are under the authority of the dominant power in the region, Is that dominant power the presence of God that radiates from you?

Perhaps it is time to start prayer-walking your neighborhood, soaking it in God's love and staking out the territory for the angels to move in and begin their work of ministering to those who would inherit salvation.

Perhaps it is time to move from intercessory prayer to intercessory action and step out to meet the needs in your community. After all, the greatest command is this: to love the Lord, and your neighbor.

If you want an exponential increase of power in your life, cultivate love.

## Endnotes

1. For more information about Karen Berner and Jeannie Fuller's prayer journey, see—www.thelibertyprayer.blogspot.com.

2. Watchman Nee, *The Normal Christian Life*, Christian Classics Ethereal Library, *http://www.ccel.org/ccel/nee/normal.xviii.ii.html* (accessed December 1, 2011).

3. For more information about James Goll and the Encounters Network, visit www.encountersnetwork.com.

Chapter Eight

# FROM AMBASSADOR'S ANOINTING TO APOSTOLIC POWER

Faithfulness to live the normal Christian life filled with the presence and power of God that compels you to minister to individuals before you, brings increase, as James Goll just pointed out to us in the previous chapter. Along with that increase, a greater anointing of authority and power is released. Eventually, some realize that the normal Christian life has just taken them a quantum leap into another *metron*, or sphere of influence. I call this the "Ambassador's Anointing," an anointing that also includes "consuls." Those who step into this do so after much training and faithfulness. Their character has been tested and tried through the fires of life, and their ability to perceive what God is doing and understand His heart for nations (rather than individuals) has become a governmental and apostolic ministry focused on reconciliation.

In diplomatic terms, an ambassador is the foreign diplomatic representative of a nation who is authorized to handle political negotiations between his or her country and the country where the ambassador has been assigned. A consul is the commercial agent of a nation who is empowered only to engage in business transactions, and not political matters in the country where he or she is stationed. The President, with the consent of the Senate, appoints ambassadors and consuls.

In God's Kingdom, an ambassador is anyone who is in the ministry of reconciling others to God. But Paul hints at a greater level of authority when he addresses the Corinthians:

> For Christ's love compels us, because we are convinced that one died for all, and therefore all died. And He died for all, that those who live should no longer live for themselves but for Him who died for them and was raised again.

> So from now on we regard no one from a worldly point of view. Though we once regarded Christ in this way, we do so no longer. Therefore, if anyone is in Christ, he is a new creation; the old has gone, the new has come! All this is from God, who reconciled us to Himself through Christ and gave us the ministry of reconciliation: that God was reconciling the world to Himself in Christ, not counting men's sins against them. And He has committed to us the message of reconciliation. We are therefore Christ's ambassadors, as though God were making His appeal through us. We implore you on Christ's behalf: Be reconciled to God. God made Him who had no sin to be sin for us, so that in Him we might become the righteousness of God (2 Corinthians 5:14-21).

All are anointed as ambassadors, but some are anointed for specific tasks and offices. Paul was not speaking as an everyday believer. Paul spoke as an elder with an apostolic authority and anointing. The ambassador's anointing is also apostolic. Some are being reconciled to God; others are calling for the reconciliation. They are ambassadors of

the King and apostles, prophets, priests, or pastors—those who operate in a governmental authority in the process. The political, economic,
and spiritual realms of God's authority are not given to just anyone.

It was customary to anoint kings, prophets, and priests during
their inauguration ceremony as they entered into their office. The
word "anoint" is applied to priests in Exodus 28:41; 40:15. It is applied
to prophets in First Kings 19:16; Isaiah 61:1. It is applied to a king in
First Samuel 10:1; 15:1; Second Samuel 2:4; and First Kings 1:34.

It is applied often to the Messiah who was set apart or consecrated
to His office as prophet, priest, and king—making Him the only one
appointed by God to the highest office ever held in the world. It is
applied also to Christians who are consecrated or set apart to the service of God by the Holy Spirit. Who is qualified? Every believer who
sets himself or herself apart for ministry has greater potential than
he or she ever dreamed possible. The supernatural anointing creates
something sacred and powerful out of the ordinary.

We see individuals setting themselves apart to wait on the Lord and
receive an anointing of the Holy Spirit in Acts 2 when the Holy Spirit
was poured out upon the believers who were gathered in the Upper
Room. Apparently, those initial believers were Jews who believed that
Jesus was the Messiah, because in Acts 10 we see Peter astonished that
the Holy Spirit later extended the range of His anointing—*"The circum-
cised believers who had come with Peter were astonished that the gift of the
Holy Spirit had been poured out even on the Gentiles"* (Acts 10:45).

Jew and Gentile were solemnly set apart, and consecrated to the
service of God. But the Jews were first in the anointing line. Gentiles
were grafted in later. We don't know what those who were gathered in
the Upper Room did with the Holy Spirit after they left. We really only
know of the disciples turned apostles. Some who were mentioned in
the Book of Acts may have become house church leaders and prophets
and prophetesses. Some, perhaps, were evangelists. The point is they
came out of their encounter very different from when they went in.

Peter was one of the first who received an ambassador's anointing. His call was to reconcile Jew and Gentile, and he realized this in Acts 10 after he encountered Cornelius.

> *Then Peter began to speak: "I now realize how true it is that God does not show favoritism but accepts men from every nation who fear Him and do what is right"* (Acts 10:34-35).

> *While Peter was still speaking these words, the Holy Spirit came on all who heard the message. The circumcised believers who had come with Peter were astonished that the gift of the Holy Spirit had been poured out even on the Gentiles. For they heard them speaking in tongues and praising God.*

> *Then Peter said, "Can anyone keep these people from being baptized with water? They have received the Holy Spirit just as we have." So he ordered that they be baptized in the name of Jesus Christ...* (Acts 10:44-48).

Part of the ambassador's anointing is the call to reconcile all believers into one new man in Christ. It is a calling to unify the Body—the original nation of Israel, the first nations tribes of the world, and all those who were grafted in through the centuries or could be grafted in, including Muslims and peoples of other faiths who recognize Jesus as Messiah.

## The Ambassador's Anointing

Those who carry the ambassador's anointing are appointed by the Holy Spirit to serve as His representative at high-level meetings in various nations. They are special envoys whose authority is directly connected to the highest offices of state with a defined mission of reconciliation. Their anointing comes supernaturally, and they realize that their encounter with God released the vision setting them apart to reach the nations and imparted both a commissioning to the task and an impartation of power to carry out the mission. They are not new believers. They have been tested, tried, and refined. Ambassadors

✕

receive special training that provides the foundation for the finesse they will need in such a political role.

Myles Weiss is one who has stepped into an ambassador's anointing in recent years. You probably have not heard of him. Most ambassadors are not platform people. They serve in hidden places. Part of Myles' training involved his work as a marriage and family counselor where he helped people become reconciled to God and one another. Along the way, Myles dramatically encountered God and found himself getting in touch with his Jewish roots, and received the commission to reconcile nations. His secular training became invaluable as it worked synergistically with the gifts of the Spirit to release God's purposes in lives. Today he is a therapist, leader of Beth Shalom, a thriving Messianic congregation in Northern California, and a Messianic Jew who speaks around the world, reconciling many, from all religious backgrounds, to the God of Abraham, Isaac, and Jacob.[1]

What follows is an interview that explains the process God took him through and where he is going in the future. I write about him because anti-Semitism is still so prevalent in our culture. We also need deeper understanding of the sons of Ishmael. We need ambassadors of reconciliation to release the peace and keep the peace. Only anointed men and women of God can reach those who are so hurt and wounded on a generational and nationalistic level. Only men and women anointed as ambassadors can call the Church to understand and embrace the nations of Israel and Arab states. Myles is one.

## What is your definition of the anointing?

My definition of the anointing is to see what God is seeing, to be in concert with what He's doing in the moment. So is He healing physically, is He touching inner life, is He releasing His life? It's wherever He's bringing the Kingdom in a person or in a circumstance. It's wherever the Kingdom of Heaven is coming to affect someone. I was just looking at some work I'm doing for writing and people asking, "If Messiah has come, why is the world in such a mess?" And the answer is, it's not a mess where His anointing is, where His Kingdom has come in individuals, congregations, or families. You can see something of Heaven, something of the fruit of the anointing. So I would say it's the release of His life—capital H—His life into a person or circumstance.

## So there is an alignment with Him that needs to take place for breakthrough to happen?

Absolutely and that's why this seeming unsolvable mystery of the war between the Jews and the Arabs, the sons of Isaac and the sons of Ishmael, continues on. You see wherever a Jewish person or an Arab person comes into a real faith, leans into and believes into and surrenders to the anointing of the Messiah as King, there is peace between them. Yeshua is "Sar Shalom," the "Prince of Peace." It is a very satisfying part of our work. I'm actually working with a local Arab pastor doing services together and speaking to all the Bay Area leaders who are connected with the Bethel river movement. During one of the morning sessions, Pastor Ziad and I will have the chance to bring the message of reconciliation [by] modeling a living testimony of an Arab and a Jew standing together in Christ.

## Just that visual testimony is powerful in itself.

We had a practice run a few weeks ago at a local church, and at the end there was weeping all around and the Jews ended up praying for the Arabs and the Arabs for the Jews. God just broke through and healed people of years, or decades, or generations, of anti-Semitism, or in our modern world, "anti-Arabism."

We have both anti-Semitism and anti-Arabism in our country. And some people would relate that to principalities and powers over a country. However, one person who comes in humbly and anointed with the presence of the Lord for reconciliation can do some incredible work in people's hearts and minds.

You think of Jesus, who came as one; then there were 12, then 11, then 12 again; this small group of people called disciples. I believe now that wherever my friend and I put the soles of our feet, wherever they tread, God will bring His Kingdom of peace. We will experience righteousness, peace, and joy in the Holy Spirit!

## Now you started to talk about reconciliation between Jew, Arab, and Christian. Why is that important?

Well, I think it is a sign of the times. Jesus said to His Jewish disciples, "You'll not see Me again until you say, 'Baruch ha bah B'Shem Adonai'" (*blessed is He who comes in the name of* ✗ *the Lord*). And so the time clock of the restoration of Israel has something to do with the return of the Lord. There are different theories about what that means, what a generation is, etc. But it is significant. You can trace actual history, following the outbreak of the movements of the modern Church from the late 1800s and early 1900s right up to our day. You can track increase in the Church, which parallels the restoration of Israel and the Jewish people. It's a phenomenal study; it's actually on my website if you want to look at it (www.visitbethshalom.org).

There is something that God is doing in concert with this restoration of His natural brethren to the land, to their place, fulfilling their destiny in the land, which will lead to coming into the Spirit and looking for the Messiah. Our cousins, our brothers, who are intended to be our brothers in the Lord, the sons of Ishmael, must also humbly enter the Kingdom of God through the finished work of Messiah. It becomes a mark of the power of God, the love of God, and the ability of God to bring Heaven to earth when there is reconciliation between Jews and Arabs, to former Muslims and the Body at large. Former Muslims who love Jesus, His Jewish family, and the Jewish place in the land are modern heroes. They understand that they have been "grafted in" to the commonwealth of Israel, according to Ephesians, chapter 2.

## Where there is unity and reconciliation, peace happens.

Psalm 133 says, "Behold, how good and how pleasant it is when the brethren dwell together in unity. It is like the oil on Aaron's beard that flows down through his garments all the way to his feet." And it's there it says at the end of the psalm that He commands life forevermore. The blessing is commanded: life forevermore. God takes it very seriously.

## Do you believe that it's not just speaking about unity among like-minded believers; it's talking about Arab, Jew, Christian, and all nations?

That's exactly right; that's a really, really good word and a very important insight. I work among several groups of pastors, especially in two counties of the U.S. Here, we think of unity as a goal because of our denominationalism and our various stripes of Christianity and we think, *Oh when we get unity, won't it be great.* I came in low; I came in serving their congregations as a therapist and gaining their trust and being a part of the crowd, but once I got them connected to Israel, and they saw what it's like to be connected to that living root of the Messianic world, they started to understand that unity is not a goal, it's an entrance requirement, it's a starting point.

✘

Paul said in Ephesians, endeavor *"...to keep the unity of the Spirit in the bond of peace"* (Eph. 4:3), he didn't say attain to it, or strive after it because of your denominations. He said if you're walking in divisions, you're walking as natural men and I can't even speak to you as spiritual. So it's really a beginning. Unity is step one. There's a step program in the return of the Lord. Step one—we are in unity in the Spirit now; let's reach across to the really difficult, difficult places. You know it's a celebration whenever the Church gets together, but how much cooler when ethnic barriers and long-held divisions are broken down by the power of the Lord? It's awesome.

## How did God call you into the ministry of reconciling nations?

In our own journey, we started out serving in a large missions-minded work that held distinctive large Gospel meetings wherever we went. We ministered in India, Africa, and Russia with a focus on salvation and healing on a massive scale. I was a setup guy and a video guy, a "carry the luggage" guy, who was just really serving and seeing God do incredible things. Occasionally, my traveling buddy was an Arab. So we would come into a city in India, or a place in the backwaters of India, or Africa, and we would say to the Catholics, the Charismatics, Baptists, Pentecostals, and the denominations that we are going to lift up the name of Jesus for a week. *There will be salvation and healing and deliverance, and pastors are going to move forward in their ministries. There will be breakthrough on every level and we are all going to get along together. You know how we know that? Because he's an Arab from Ramallah and I'm a New York Jew. If we can get along, you can get along!*

It's amazing how that opened the door for not only the local pastors to reach for the entrance requirement of unity, but also it worked on me because God gave me love for my Arab brother, and he for me. We had to work some things out along the way, as you can imagine. We had to work out loving this person, whom the media, the cultures, the history, the current events were all telling us was impossible.

One day I'm on my way back from conducting marriage seminars in Russia with my wife when a young, prophetic man said, "You're cheating your kids out of their heritage." And so we said how? "Well, you're a Jew; you need to teach them where they came from. Not just serving the nations and doing what you're doing, but you need to also tell them something about the blessing of Abraham."✗

So that set us on a journey of holding Shabbat on a regular basis and celebrating the feasts in our home. Israelis were showing up, old folks were coming; all these people that would never set foot in a church were coming into our home. Eventually, about 80 people were showing up. One night, a 96-year-old man got saved in my kitchen. He started weeping and wondering what's going on, "What's happening to me? I haven't felt this way since my wife died. I have felt so alone until tonight. What's different, what's going on?"

And I said to him, "Your soul is being saved, Max. God is saving you and drawing [you] to the Mashiach, to the Messiah. You're in contact with the God of Abraham, Isaac, and Jacob. He's changing you." When I walked him out to his car and knelt down to say goodbye, he strained to tell me that his neck was in severe pain. I prayed a simple prayer and God healed his neck. So the Kingdom had come to him, to Max, in my kitchen. And the meetings grew. So when it became too big for our home, we began to meet in churches and in other places, and along the way this reconciliation with my Arab cousins and brothers became a central part of what we do. And I was connecting to the root in Israel, to the people that are laboring there on the front lines. We

found Arab Christians and Jewish believers living together
𝗑 in the peace of the Messiah. The body of Messianic believers
in Israel is a heroic community and it's grown tremendously
over the past few decades.

**There is something about you returning to your Israeli roots
or your Jewish roots and reconnecting with your heritage
that released an even greater anointing and direction and
calling to reconciliation.**

Absolutely; it completely changed the direction of my life. I
spent two weeks on Mount Carmel with David and Karen
Davis and Peter Tsukahira's ministry there. I went up to
Mount Carmel and wept for two weeks as God reordered my
DNA around my Hebrew roots. It resulted in my thirst to see
this message get out to the Body in the Bay Area of California
and beyond; and it's absolutely transformative. Since early
2000 I've received an endless revelation about the ministry of
reconciliation. I never get tired of it. I never lose energy about
it. I get discouraged, but I've never looked back in terms of
the direction of our ministry.

**So you had your strong God encounter that set you off on
this commissioning.**

Yes, for sure. And along the way there's been great encour-
agement. Cindy Jacobs has spoken over us; Chuck Pierce
ordained us; and Bill Johnson had a word for us. Ed Silvoso
adopted me, and there's been a lot of favor with established
believers. This last November, Ed Silvoso had me bring the
message of the "One New Man" to almost 700 world leaders. They were marketplace, Church, and government leaders who gathered in Hawaii for a transformation conference
and he had me bring the message of reconciliation to the
whole group. The highlight was when I showed a DVD clip
of an Arab Pastor from Carmel who tells a little bit of his

story. At the end of the movie, Ed Silvoso took off his shoes, got up on the platform, and admonished everyone to take off their shoes as they were standing on holy ground. When you see what God is doing, calling the sons of Ishmael back to the God of Abraham, you experience the holiness of His purposes.

God's economy is humorous that He is using a Jew to do that. Our ministry is focused on raising up the Church as Esther, to stand in the gap for God's people. This includes those that know Him and those who do not yet know Him. In a typically Jewish comical note…my given Hebrew name happens to be Mordecai!

**Have you noticed in churches that those who have no grid for understanding our connection with Israel, the Christian connection with Ha Eretz, lack in the anointing? And those who bless Israel see an increase in anointing? Or nations for that matter?**

That's a very good question because there are many that don't have any grid at all and yet there is an anointing and there is breakthrough. In fact, some of them are leaders in revival. So I had a controversy with the Lord about five years ago where I said, "What's the story here, God?" I'm doing my best and preaching this everywhere I go. I'm taking about 250 pastors to Israel and they say things like 'Myles, why wasn't this taught 25 years ago in seminary? Why did I wait my whole life to learn this?'" They get this incredible revelation of what the Bible says in Genesis 12:1-3, "I will bless those that bless you and curse those who curse you." And that word "curse" means to esteem lightly; like if you don't get into this, there's a loss. The Lord said, "Myles, they are the beneficiaries of my restoration of Israel whether they know it or not."

Implied in that was that this movement of restoration that God's doing in the Body worldwide and has been doing for centuries, of restoring different aspects of His life and His anointing, is increasing and will move on. You can do it without this connection, but my contention is that God wants us to do it on purpose, in connection. He wants the messianic to be connected to the revivalists, so we don't get dry and liturgical. And He wants the revivalists to honor the Jewish root because it is right to do so and God has a double blessing for all of us.

**Do you think when some of the revival leaders get a hold of this they will see an exponential increase in power and anointing?**

Yes, that is what I believe. We need the oil of the Gentiles and the oil of the Jews to fill the candelabra. It's two becoming one. It's the two olive trees in Zechariah and it's this mystery of Ephesians 2—God breaking down the wall. Even with the incredible things we are seeing in the earth today, how much more will we see when we are living out of Psalm 133, living unity on purpose, intentionally?

## From Ambassadors to Apostolic Anointing

There are those who move in the authority of the Lord, releasing an ambassadorial anointing to move hearts, change minds, and reconcile individuals to God and nations to one another. Some release both the authority and the power to back up their words with signs and wonders. That increase of power shifts them into another level of anointing—apostolic anointing.

In *Shifting Shadows of Supernatural Power*, I wrote about the convergence of the healing and prophetic movements and gifts. As we move onwards and upwards, most people in ministry recognize that the two are so intertwined that new language has emerged to contain the amount of power for miracles that is coming forth from many ministries. It is called *apostolic* and rightly so. For the word "apostolic" means "sent one" and implies that the one sent has all the authority and power to back up his or her words. Those who are carrying the anointing to regions and nations must move in apostolic power for miracles, signs, and wonders to break through hearts and shatter principalities and powers over regions. Jesus is more easily embraced when we learn how to move in sync with Him and when our words are backed up by demonstrations of power.

Rather than the anointing being limited to a handful of forerunners, many believe that the soon-to-come outpouring of the Holy Spirit will release an apostolic anointing to thousands of people around the world. We are seeing young leaders emerging in many countries who release God's healing power and presence with apostolic anointing and wisdom that seem beyond their years. They are the emerging forerunners of their nations. But many more are still to come. Those who move in both the ambassadorial anointing and apostolic anointing are the emerging history-makers, transforming nations and making disciples of all nations.

Randy Clark[2] is one who has learned to walk in his anointing and impart that anointing to others through power encounters that launched ministries to the nations. A Baptist minister turned Vineyard pastor, Randy had an encounter with the Lord that empowered him to launch a ministry of world significance. Randy Clark birthed his ministry, Global Awakening, in January 1994 as a result of God using him to bring the fire of revival to the Toronto Airport Christian Fellowship. That revival was considered the greatest revival movement of the last half of the 20th Century, a move of God resulting in the longest protracted meeting in the history of North America.

During the first year, the "Blessing," as it became known, spread to 55,000 churches around the world. Over three million people visited the church during the first few years, with thousands being rededicated and saved, and thousands more empowered and equipped to minister more effectively.

Today, over a decade later, as a result of Randy's ministry in Toronto and around the world, between 6,000 and 7,000 churches have been started in Mozambique. This has resulted in about one million new believers coming into the Kingdom of God. The revival in Mozambique was birthed through a prophetic word Randy gave Heidi Baker in Toronto, accompanied by a powerful impartation of the Holy Spirit. The fire of this move of God in Toronto spread through Iris Ministries, launched by Rolland and Heidi Baker, to the mission field of Mozambique. From there it has already spread to over ten African nations and is rapidly spreading around the world as Iris Ministries exponentially increases on other continents.

In addition to the revival in Mozambique, the fire of the Toronto move of God is touching other nations. In 1995, Randy prayed and prophesied over the Norwegian pastor Leif Hetland, another minister whose life was radically changed. A powerful impartation of the Holy Spirit came upon Leif when he received the prophetic word from Randy. Since then, Leif has been used to bring more than a million people, many of them Muslims, into the Kingdom of God, and he has helped establish over a thousand "Lighthouses of Love" in Pakistan and the Middle East.

I interviewed Randy about his definition of the anointing and the ability to impart the anointing to create history makers and world changers.

## How is it that God has used you to impart such anointing to others?

Apostolic leaders often carry an anointing for impartation but they also carry the anointing so that others would be healed and filled with the Holy Spirit. Impartation is one of the main ways God uses me to bring people up to a new level of anointing, usually for healing.

## Was there a specific moment when you realized you had received a specific anointing for the mandate/mission/office given you?

My first call was the call to preach at 18 years old, and that came through three signs. One sign the Lord gave me came through my cousin, who hated Christians and didn't go to church. I prayed that God would save him. That day he got saved. I also prayed that God would give me a different, specific sign. I had been reading about Moses at the time so I said, "If You have called me to preach, then give me the sign of a tree burning." Later, someone was burning trash and from where I stood, I thought a tree was on fire. The final sign that caused me to embrace my call to preach was the healing of a youth pastor who couldn't play piano after a stroke. I prayed for him, and when his hands hit the keys he was healed without any further pain.

The call on my life has evolved since then. After 1984, during my initial experience with the Vineyard Movement, I felt the power of God with shaking and electricity running through my body for the first time. My joints all ached the next day from the amount of the power I felt. Then, in 1989, I experienced the most powerful impartation of anointing. It lasted 45 minutes with electricity laying me out on the floor to the point where I couldn't move. In the meanwhile, I received several important prophetic words from others. I had been asking God what I am to be used for. The anointing seemed too strong. Bob Jones said I had a teaching gift. John Wimber said it was healing.

Ron Allen, regional overseer for the Vineyard from Ohio, told me one day that the enemy had tried to kill my son because of strong anointing in his life. He said, "You will travel the nations when you are older, and your son will travel with you, but he will not ride your coattails." That is still unfolding.

**So you had the call to preach, teach, heal, and go to the nations. When did you sense that you were commissioned and released?**

In 1993, I went to a Rodney Howard Browne meeting and got a powerful touch. I had him pray for me five or six times. When I came home, someone saw the Shekinah glory all over church. After that, everywhere I went people started to shake and get healed. I asked God for the anointing for healing. I also asked to be one of the thousand people that Rodney Howard Browne heard would take it all over the world. Not long after, I was invited to Toronto because John Arnott had heard that the power of God was coming into my church.

**Under the umbrella of your anointing, people on ministry trips with you see results when they pray for others that they don't see at home. How do you explain these phenomena? Are they operating under a situational anointing?**

It is a general anointing.

People I lay hands on generally receive an impartation. Some people receive strengthening in their gifts. Once when I was ministering, Bonnie Chavda saw hundreds of angels strengthening pastors. However, she only saw three people who were being ministered to by angels reading from a scroll, declaring what a person's destiny was, and imparting the power to carry it out.

Most everyone is strengthened in the Holy Spirit and the gifts but a few receive the commissions—the impartation unto a new office. It is a different impartation. So when I leave, or the people leave the ministry trip, it doesn't end. They stay at a higher level of anointing to heal. It is a sovereign call from the Lord. Not everyone is apostolic, or a healing evangelist, or prophetic. God chooses and calls.

## Do we limit the anointing or are we limited by our own understanding?

Be careful of limiting God. But there are different anointings for different seasons of time for what you are called to do. It is not like there is one anointing.

## What does it take to become a history-maker and walk in apostolic anointing?

There are three keys to becoming history-makers:

1) They have a powerful experience or encounter with the Lord,

2) They have an understanding of what that experience is unto—the meaning, purpose, and destiny. And then understanding that destiny enables the third thing...

3) They won't quit no matter what happens. The understanding is so strong they won't give up. The encounter they had creates a persevering grace and persevering faith.

In Heidi Baker, if it had just been that she received a word about her destiny alone, without power so strong that she could never doubt the word, no matter what the devil did against her, I don't know if she would have made it. [In] the next 18 months following her amazing encounter with God during a meeting in Toronto, she lost her financial support, experienced severe health issues, her kids had issues, the ministry went into severe financial troubles, and there was opposition against her in the country that God had originally anointed her to occupy. But she could not doubt the word because the manifestation of God was so strong.

## The Anointing That Changes the World

Heidi and Rolland Baker, founders of Iris Ministries,[3] have been missionaries primarily known for their work in Mozambique. They are also known and loved around the world for the work Iris Ministries missionaries have done: seeking and saving the lost, feeding the poor, releasing miracles of healing, and raising the dead, and signs and wonders like multiplying food sources—supernaturally and naturally—as well as walking as ambassadors of God's love. Heidi is one who carries the anointing that changes the world. She walks in power multiplied by love and a sound mind (good judgment, sobriety, and wise discretion). The result is an apostolic anointing that changes the world.

I interviewed Heidi Baker while she was in a hotel room in Seoul, Korea, after a series of meetings she ministered in; meetings that could likely tip the balance of power in North Korea and tumble the nations into a unified embrace in the Father's love. I asked her about the progression of her anointing and how she increased in her anointing to change the world.

**Do you say what happened with you in Toronto years ago was a time of incredible anointing and increase that just changed everything?[6]**

For me it had a lot to do with the Father's heart. I've always been really passionate for Jesus and I've spent hours with

Him since I was saved. I've always been really intimate with Him, but this understanding that Father's there, that I can just lean back into His presence, in His arms, and He'll come through, shifts the whole way you minister. It's out of a security in Him that you minister. You're dependent on Holy Spirit totally, but you are sure Daddy is going to show up for you.

## Was that the shift that happened to you when God was ministering to you in Toronto?

That was the main thing that happened—the shift in His security and knowing that He is going to come through. I also shifted into more rest, feeling like I don't have to strive so much. I still fast obviously, but back then I fasted one third of my life. Until a few years ago, I felt like I had to earn the favor somehow. And now it's like Daddy loves me and it's OK to eat sometimes; it's OK to rest sometimes; it's OK to take a day off once in awhile. That's a whole new place for me.

## The breakthrough happened in you first, but then how did it happen in the land?

Well, mostly by hearing God speak to me over and over that it's His job to heal and it's my job to love; and that I need to be secure in who I am in Him. I started really listening to the rhythm of His heart to run, to rest, to release. It was about learning how to release, instead of me trying to make it happen with Him. Then, instead of me doing the work and pushing and striving and leading, I was able to hear Him say, "Release this one." I started seeing an increase of miracles and growth as I released sons and daughters. I was so secure in who I was that I could release it to a generation.

## As you released it, God gave you more?

Yes, it was releasing it to little ones, telling them they could see the deaf hear and the blind see and the dead get raised. And I released, I released, I released them and had no desire to be seen and God began to multiply. You know 12 guys went out and started ministering in the Bible, but only 3 of them raised the dead. God started using little children and everything shifted.

## So that's one way to increase the anointing, propagate it.

Yeah, give it away. Out of control, release control. That's my biggest word—release control.

## Can you talk a little bit about that progression of encounter and release and following Him where He is taking you?

Yeah, that was a real sovereign, divine thing. When I was in my 20s, I had some ambition and really wanted to speak to the nations and in the stadiums and in the big meetings, which I was doing. One day in my 20s, the Lord said, "Stop!" He said three times to stop. He told me to sit with the poor and learn about the Kingdom. So I did that for probably 18 years or 20 years. I lived in the slums with the poor, learning about dependence, learning about living a life that is needy; needing and desperate every day, not just for myself, but for all my friends. My friends were the poor.

Then, after encountering God in Toronto, it shifted. I never dreamed or wanted to speak to the Western Church or the Eastern Church. I just wanted to hide myself as I had been doing for 20 some years among the poor and be hidden.

Then one day, after a year of praying for the blind (you know that story from one of my books), they started to see. God opened the first woman's eyes, and her name was Mama Aida (Heidi in Portuguese). I watched her eyes go white, grey, and then brown. Then the next day, I prayed for a man and he didn't see, which was really interesting.

The next day, I prayed for a woman and she was miraculously healed and her eyes opened. She'd been blind since she was eight and she began to scream and she could see and I took her to the village and all the villagers came around and started yelling and dancing and saying, *"Mama Aida can see."* Well, that's my name in Mozambique as well, Mama Aida. Day three leads to such an extraordinary story. I called the blind to the meeting and there was only one blind lady in the meeting, so she came and I prayed for her. She fell on the ground and her eyes went white, grey, brown. And everybody started dancing and screaming and praising and saying, *"Mama Aida can see, Mama Aida can see."* That woman's name was also Mama Aida. Is that the wildest thing you ever heard? Three women with my name getting healed of blindness over three days?

So, I mean I'd never seen a blind person receive even a tiny sliver of light in 20 some years of ministry. I've been ministering 35 years now. So I asked God, I put my hands on my eyes and I said, "What is it? Do I have a Kathryn Kuhlman anointing? Am I Aimee Semple McPherson? Am I entering my healing, evangelistic ministry?"

And the Lord said, "You're blind."

And I said, "No, I'm a missionary."

And He said to me a second time, "You're blind."

I said, "But I work with the poor."

And a third time He said, "You're blind."

So I laid my hands on my eyes and I began to cry out, "I want to see, I want to see, Lord, let me see, let me see." When I opened my eyes I saw all these faces, like hundreds of thousands of faces. I saw Asian faces, I saw American faces, Canadian faces, and I saw young ones, too. And in these faces I saw all these different nationalities. And He said, "They are poor, they are rich, they are blind, they are naked, won't you love them, too?"

And from that day on, I said yes to going back to the Western and Asian Church that wasn't so poor as the ones I had been working with. I spend one third of my life calling people to a radical laid-down life of love and to see a missions movement rise up with those who would love the poor, love the broken, and to call the Church into greater intimacy unto fruitfulness.

**So how do you survive the anointing? You have certainly seen and heard a lot of trauma and then walked in the midst of it. And what is the secret to surviving?**

Stay low; stay low and go slow. I don't have to make myself poor in spirit because I just am, because the needs of this world and the needs of the people are so great that I stay desperate on God, desperate on Jesus. I literally come to Him, literally every moment, just poor in spirit wanting Him, dependent on Him. I stay low, I go slow, and I slow down even more when I'm not getting it right. I slow down even more, you know?

When I preach and I minister, I wait in the presence. I wait for Him. If it takes an hour or two, I'll wait that long; if it takes five hours, I'll wait that long.

**I've watched you at Bethel recently, and at other places, and it seems like such a small percentage of the people there will come forward to answer the call to love the poor and to go out and to minister to the poor. I mean it really is about maybe one percent that responds to that altar call. What do you think about? Are we just blind and hard-hearted?**

I think while everyone is called to care for children and to care for the starving and the dying in this world, there is a small percentage who are called to live among them from the Western and Eastern Church. So I'm not concerned if it's a small percentage. If I give an altar call like that, it is very specific. They are going to give their lives. I feel like every area of society needs to be influenced by the love and power and presence of God. So if someone wants to be a medical doctor, or an engineer, or professor, I see that not as a lesser value. I want the anointing to hit them as well. But the call to live and work among the poor and to rescue children out of starvation and the sex-trade industry, that is a specific call, and the reason I can call them in is because I live that. And while I can call the whole Church into intimacy unto fruitfulness, I can call this small, small group that God is literally calling to this.

**When I see them come and respond and I see you pray, it's like there is transference of that grace that you have on your life. So maybe just one percent, but I see how broken they are instantly by the Holy Spirit. Instantly the grace comes and it's imparted at that time.**

Yeah, and they are all over the world. They might be a tiny percentage in a meeting, but there are hundreds of them all over the world, living in the slums, bringing home the child slaves, caring for the most desperate people and that is beautiful to me.

I don't think it's everyone's call. I think everyone should adopt at least one child and feed one child, I mean in a sponsorship kind of program. I think every Christian should do that. I can't imagine a Christian not doing that, not caring for one child, and some are called to give up their whole lives.

**What do you sense about the anointing that is coming? In your travels around the world are you seeing hints to come of God's fresh outpouring?**

I do. Everywhere we go I see people getting completely wrecked. But I feel like God wants to bring this radical love revolution where people start focusing on loving the one right in front of them, and it's more about carrying love everywhere than it's about a meeting.

This movement that I'm praying for is a love revolution where Christians are actually known by their love wherever they are in society, wherever they move, wherever they walk. It's all about breathing, smelling, and walking like Jesus, not so much about a meeting in a certain place. It's like carrying His presence, the glory of His love out, into every single part of society. People don't have to ask who you believe in because of the way you treat people and care for people; they can see who you believe in. Christians are known by their love. And I feel like God is ripping anger out of people, and depression, and fear, and causing them to live a life of radical love. That's what I'm seeing. That's what I'm longing for.

**How do people get there? Do they just have to be open to it and say yes to the Lord and just go for it?**

Yes, and it's also sovereign when God takes our little hearts and makes them bigger. I'd say it's actually a gift. I believe

199

that you know. He did it for me in Toronto, and He continues to do it for us. There's something that when God does that, when He comes crashing in on you in a sovereign way in a meeting, then He totally takes away hatred and anger, and allows you to forgive people who have hurt you and ridiculed you. Once that happens—you change. But then you have to live that life out. So I believe that we need more of those kinds of meetings where the presence is so strong that God literally rips out the hardness of our hearts and puts His heart in us. That's what I'm longing for, more of those meetings. I saw it yesterday [the day before the interview]. I saw South Koreans come up and instead of just writhing and shaking to receive the anointing and wanting the woman or man of power to touch them, they were on their faces sobbing their guts out, and God was giving them such a huge taste of His heart of love for them and others.

Receiving the heart of the Lord for the nations is an invitation to feel what He feels for the lost and broken of the world. God's love opens hearts and His power shatters their bondage. Love and power seem to be the key markers of the apostolic anointing carried by people like Heidi Baker and Leif Hetland. It enables them to persevere against opposition and not be moved by what they see with their eyes and run away in fear. Keeping their focus on God, who is love, enables them to cast aside fears for their own safety and move into the darkest places where opposition often becomes violent.

Leif Hetland is the founder of Global Missions Awareness. I wrote about him in a previous chapter. A young Norwegian pastor when he encountered God dramatically during a Randy Clark meeting, he soon shifted into a commissioning accompanied by apostolic power to take the nations.

**When you go out into these deep dark places, like Pakistan, you're facing men with guns and so much resistance that you need to be secure in knowing that God had called you to that assignment and that you have the anointing to carry it out.**[7]

I think that there's connection with anointing and assignment. So my assignment of reaching the unreached, of taking the gospel to the darkest places in the world—to the places where there's never been any good news—is a special anointing. Walking into the room, changing the environment, and to be able to do signs, wonders, and miracles just flows very naturally.

But, if I go in a different setting I am not anointed for, it would be like me trying to fix a car. Then I become very annoying. The difference between "anointed" and "annoying" is a very big difference. That has to do with assignment.

I have to make sure that there is a major grace involved that is connected to the assignment. The other thing I think we need is to be free from fear. Jesus says, "I have not given you a spirit of fear, but what I have given you is a spirit of power, and love, and a sound mind." I think one of the first major freedoms connected to the anointing is that I had to become free from fear.

The other thing I think has to do with worldview—how you perceive or see things. Are you seeing it from Heaven's perspective? When the anointing is there, when I look at Islam I don't see Islam as a problem. I see it as a promise. And you can only receive a promise. When I am looking at somebody that is full of hatred, all I see is that they have never experienced His love. So I am seeing them through Heaven's eyes.

Saul, who became the apostle Paul, was the first terrorist named in the New Testament. He terrorized Stephen. So, when I'm looking at a solid terrorist, I see the apostle Paul. That's what the anointing did. So, when you are there [in a Muslim country] and you're seeing somebody that wants to cut your throat, or you see "honor" killing—you see some of the most gruesome stuff—you have to be able to see with the eyes of Jesus.

I mean, they've got bad news. I've got good news. Who's going to win? "The Spirit of the Lord is upon me and He has anointed me." Wherever there is darkness, I've got light. Where there is sadness, I can have oil of gladness.

So when I say, "If Christ Jesus, that is the Anointed One, if He is here and if He is alive, and He is in me, you are going to see these things. And I declare you're going to see blind eyes opened, deaf and mute hearing, tumors are going to fall off people—you're going to see it." And they do.

## What's the most amazing meeting or series of meetings that God has used you in?

I think the most amazing meeting I have ever seen was recently, when we were in Pakistan. In America I've seen the whole environment change, but I think what made this meeting very unique for me was the place we were at. We literally saw the environment change and I had never seen such a transformation. It took three days, but by that Sunday service we saw so many creative miracles—in the thousands— that I've never seen anything like it. I've seen miracles, but the hunger level was intense. The people thought—because they'd never heard of Jesus or known anything about Jesus— that Jesus was me.

They were storming the police cars with guns and machine guns trying to get to us, and I have video clips of this. But they came up trying to touch you, carrying their half-dead children, hoping that if they could just touch you they were going to get well.

There was this girl who you could see there was nothing in her eyes—she had been born with no eyeballs—and I saw them bringing her up closer. And the closer she got to the presence of God you could see the creative miracle taking place. I have a picture of myself standing up there. They actually handed me this girl—who was seven or eight years old—and you could see she received eyeballs. She could see for the first time. She looks out at the thousands of people in the audience, she'd look into your face and then grin and just smile, and you know the anointing has broken her yoke.

Then her family told all their friends—so an explosiveness of power and faith occurred. But the biggest thing was just the environment change. Literally, when we left there you could feel the environment had changed. We went into a place where there has never been light, a totally unreached area. Probably, I don't know, thousands and thousands of people prayed and received Jesus, night after night.

What I've been after is not to have just a visitation, but to create an environment one day where we can change the atmosphere. Then we can be not just a thermometer; we can be a thermostat. I mean, that's what the anointing is doing. It's going in and changing the temperature that is in a room.

That's probably the meeting that I will never forget. I have hundreds of meetings where I've seen amazing things, but there was something there that—I really saw Heaven come down and change everything.

## What do you see coming in the future of missions?

I think that the major shift that is coming has to do with the unwise and the wise virgins. There are going to be ten virgins in the end time, according to Matthew 25. But five of them will end wise. All ten of them had lamps. They all had ministries—maybe for some ministries to nations. The biggest shift I see taking place in regard to the anointing is that we are moving from the old system, where you can burn the wick and run from conferences to places and seminars and purchase anointing oil. The shift that's taking place in regard to the anointing is going to be the realization that you're going to have to burn brightly without burning out. The only way to do that is to obtain the oil of intimacy for yourself.

Also, when it comes to missions, what we have done is we tried to achieve something you only can receive. "Ask of me and I will give it to you," Psalm 2:8 says. So the whole thing is about asking and receiving: "Ask of Me, and I will give you Pakistan, or ask of Me, and I will give you like what Heidi is doing in Mozambique, or the different ethno-linguistic people groups." Everything in the Kingdom can only be received, not achieved. One key to the anointing is learning to be a good receiver. ✗

There is a connection with the anointing and the presence of God where there is rest. That's how we're going to wear the enemy out, because resting is receiving. And receiving is reigning—it's ruling and reigning. So, it's only when what comes from Him goes through Him and goes back to Him will there be a flowing in the anointing. It comes from Him. It goes through Him. And it goes back to Him.

I think a major shift in the next missionary movement is going to be in identity where people realize, "I am the beloved son and daughter whom the Papa loves, in whom He is well pleased."

Lucifer was the first orphan. So when he left Heaven, he has had one major assignment—making sure people don't get home. And that's what Jesus came for. Jesus says in John 14:18, *"I will not leave you as an orphans; I will come to you."* Identity has to be the foundation of the next missionary movement. You teach what you know, but you reproduce what you are. So there's going to be impartation of identity in Him.

I think that the future's going to be full of people that obtain blueprints from Heaven. That's pretty much what the apostolic or missionary is all about, is to be able to get it from the Father and then learning how to receive it, not to achieve it.

You say, "Papa, I don't know how to do this."

And He says, "Good, then you're qualified. Then you need My anointing.

Then you have hope. You have everything else that flows from that...when the anointing is upon you. You can stand up against the opposition, because you're not conscious of the enemy trying to win; you're conscious that the Lord's already won.

## What do you think the next outpouring of God will look like?

I think there's a major love revolution coming.

And it has to be there, because it eliminates fear. Perfect love takes away fear. And believe me, it is going to be about the Father's love. Even in America, you can go in and look at statistics on the "fatherlessness" and you will find the devastation in America on a global scale. Fatherlessness is the number one root issue in the world today—even in Islam.

Randy Clark prayed for me in 1995, and I received the power and [anointing for] signs and wonders and miracles, and stadiums filled up, and all those different things. My identity used to be power, until eventually in the year 2000, when I had another encounter with the Lord, it became love and power.

Alignment with Jesus is love, and then the assignment is power. I think that there has to be [a] major love revolution. Now, everywhere I go, I make sure there is a baptism of love—people are being affirmed by the Father, and then find healing of that orphan heart and the orphan spirit; they are getting the identity of being a beloved son or daughter.

Those who walk in prophetic and apostolic anointing seem to agree that God desires to increase the level of anointing in our lives and that this anointing contains three equal components—power, love, and a sound mind. This power includes the gifts of the Spirit and the anointing specific to the assignment. Love enables us to carry the anointing to others and sustain us along the way. The sound mind is one that is free from burnout, sexual issues, and addictions. It is full of joy and peace because it is ruled by faith, hope, and love.

The coming love revolution will unleash the baptism of God's love so outrageously that many will be transformed quickly. The anointing will break the yoke and impart the healing many desperately need. Men and women will be positioned quickly into assignments reserved for them. Both Heidi Baker and Leif Hetland referred to just such God encounters in their lives—encounters that released the anointing raised to the third power, the power multiplied by love, and love multiplied by healing. The encounters released to them the understanding that they didn't have to strive, caused them to feel totally secure in the Father's love for them, and freed them from fear and past hurts and traumatic ministry situations.

These God encounters are not one-time events reserved for a special few. They are part of the magnificent relationship between you and God that continues and grows. A greater outpouring of love is coming upon you and me. I believe it. We need it. Pray it into existence.

The First Corinthians 13 definition of love also encompasses a sense of personal stability and soundness of mind. When the Spirit comes with power, we receive all the blessings of His love along with the increased power of the anointing that frees us to step into our sacred destinies. Paul writes that we can move in the gifts of the Spirit and the power of the Spirit, but without love we are nothing. Without love we gain nothing. If we are to see the anointing raised to the third power, we must come full circle and contend for God's love to awaken us once again. This is the most excellent way.

*Love is patient, love is kind. It does not envy, it does not boast, it is not proud. It is not rude, it is not self-seeking, it is not easily angered, it keeps no record of wrongs. Love does not delight in evil but rejoices with the truth. It always protects, always trusts, always hopes, always perseveres.*

*Love never fails. But where there are prophecies, they will cease; where there are tongues, they will be stilled; where there is knowledge, it will pass away. For we know in part and we prophesy in part, but when perfection comes, the imperfect disappears. When I was a child, I talked like a child, I thought like a child, I reasoned like a child. When I became a man, I put childish ways behind me. Now we see but a poor reflection as in a mirror; then we shall see face to face. Now I know in part; then I shall know fully, even as I am fully known.*

*And now these three remain: faith, hope and love. But the greatest of these is love* (1 Corinthians 13:4-13).

## Endnotes

1. For more information about Myles Weiss, go to www.visit-bethshalom.org.

3. For more information about Randy Clark, go to www.globalawakening.com.

5. For more information about Heidi and Rolland Baker, go to www.irismin.org.

Chapter Nine

# YOUR FUTURE IN GOD'S ANOINTING

The future belongs to you. You are written into the plan, but if you want to enter into His plan, you maybe have to lay aside some ideas of your own. According to many prophets and teachers, the Church is going to look very different in the years to come. The ministry of pastor, teacher, prophet, apostle, and evangelist will emerge more purely. Many who are not settled in their positions in the Kingdom will be set in place while others will be removed. You have a part to play in determining your future and the future of the anointing in your life. John Paul Jackson and Paul Keith Davis give us a glimpse of the power and authority that are emerging on the scene.

According to noted prophetic teacher and author John Paul Jackson, founder of Streams Ministries,[1] the renewing power of God and the new young leaders bringing the next generation into the Kingdom of God is coming into the Church right now. What follows is an interview with John Paul:

## What do you see the coming anointing on leadership looking like?[2]

There is a shift coming from purpose-driven leaders to presence-driven leaders. Ask yourself how much in your church can only be attributed to God's power working in your midst and that will tell you how much you are presence-focused. If you focus on prayer, not programs, you are presence-driven.

I also see a shift coming from motivational preachers to inspirational leaders. Motivational leaders produce short-term results and usually their teaching is based on fear issues. Inspirational leaders inspire people to change their lives to accomplish something. People change their life because of the leader's anointing of the Holy Spirit to empower eternal change.

The economy is changing and that will create a shift. The numbers of people attending church and the size of budgets will no longer be signs of the anointing. The hallmark of the anointing will be to change lives. Changed lives and making disciples will become the mark of a truly anointed gathering of people.

A shift is coming in the perspective of fivefold ministry. I think it will go from a financial focus to a spiritual fruit focus. We will see apostles raised up according to the Acts and Corinthians examples of fivefold anointing—not the Ephesians definition of fivefold. We will see apostles who are more interested in building up the Body of Christ rather than their own networks. True fathers, who are more than administrators, will arise. We have confused the ability to administrate for the apostolic anointing when apostles are fathers and mothers, men and women who promote their spiritual children more than themselves. They are thrilled by their son hitting more home runs than they did...not threatened by the success of their kids, but thrilled. They want their children to have children. They are anxious for the spiritual fruit of their kids to come on the scene.

When crisis comes, people are ready and longing for change. Historic models reveal prophets who repent when they make a mistake rather than spin-doctoring their words. We are coming back to that model of honesty. And we are going beyond to where the prophets will speak things and they will come to pass. A Samuel anointing will emerge—where what you say comes to pass because everything you say comes from God. Samuel focused on developing his character, and because of his character he was able to carry that level of anointing and authority.

I believe we will see evangelists who leave churches in better shape than when they came. Right now, we see many take the money and run. We don't see people come to the Lord through their ministries. Instead, we see evangelists who are in it to make a living rather than to bring souls into the Kingdom. We will see evangelists who value planting and watering, as well as the harvest. Right now, they seem to be focused on only harvest. Evangelists have devalued the planting and watering of the seed of the Kingdom. ✱

We'll see pastors who no longer see numbers of people as an indicator of their anointing. They will demand to take people where God is directing, not where the board thinks they should go. This is the end of the hurting pastors who are scared to death of board members.

211

Teachers who aren't afraid to tell people to throw away their old teaching because they were wrong will emerge as new insights come.

## Tell me about mantles in relationship to the prophetic office. Is this an Old Testament/old wineskin concept or timeless truth?

Mantles are a timeless truth. They are real. But they have been misused and abused by people saying, *I will give you my mantle*. This is not the reality of a mantle's existence. Mantles are merely an indicator of the fivefold ministry, a higher level of functioning. The overall goal of giving people a prophetic word is to get people to change what they are doing—if you do a course correction this will take place in your life. Having a prophetic mantle is that ability to speak the Word of God without predetermining how it must be said and not for the benefit of yourself.

## What are your top concerns that may inhibit the next generation from entering into the fullness of the anointing?

I always challenge my interns—don't say you are spiritual if I don't see the fruit. Does your pastor think that you are the most loving person, or growing in love, or [the] most selfish person who has no clue? I look for fruit in terms of kindness, patience, and longsuffering. That is what we should be seeing with bona fide manifestations of the Spirit.

But we're seeing so much out there that is not the focus of the Kingdom. Nowhere in Scripture has the focus of the Kingdom been on extraneous, ancillary things that happen. The focus is always on changed lives—those who have been healed, received a miracle, or raised from the dead, discover that their lives have been changed. Changed lives bear witness to the existence of the Father. One problem I see is that people are no different after their experience with God. Many are teaching people to walk on the edge of Heaven versus showing them how to get close to the throne. When you walk on the edge of Heaven you wonder, "Am I going to get in or are gates closing?" It creates anxiety and performance. We need to be teaching them how to get close to the throne and develop righteousness. ✗

We don't depend on God like we used to. Instead, we depend on the extraneous things that happen, like the diamond that falls in a meeting rather than the power of God to change lives. It is easier to believe in something impersonal than personal. God wants to prove Himself to be a very personal God, in a very impersonal world.

Paul Keith Davis is another prophetic teacher with worldwide influence. The founder of WhiteDove Ministries,[3] Paul Keith speaks about the combination of authority, power, and revelation that is coming to the Church. According to him, this power operates in a different dimension than what we are currently seeing but forerunners have given us glimpses of what is reserved for our day.

## What do you believe the next-generation anointing will look like?

The truest form of prophetic ministry is not First Corinthians 12, but Hebrews 4:12. Hebrews 4:12 speaks of the living Word, which is not a pen and parchment. It is the person of the living Word, the logos being manifested in a tangible way that removes the veil. Paul says in verse 13, *"Everything is uncovered and laid bare before the eyes of Him to whom we must give account.*" So that was what someone like William Branham ministered in. He did not minister in a First Corinthians 12 word of knowledge. When he was functioning under that anointing, the living Word, or what he called the "pillar of fire," would come, and literally it was like pulling a curtain back between the two realms. In that place, what you have is an entirely different dimension, a greater realm of authority. So in that place, there is complete accuracy. That's the Samuel anointing. That is what I believe we are coming into.

The Bible says that none of Samuel's words fell to the ground (see 1 Sam. 3:19). When Branham ministered under that anointing, he was always correct. Even his worst critics said that. So that's my standard, and anything short of that is a little bit disappointing. I'm convinced we can get there. I believe the sons of the Kingdom will get there.

## So what would it look like today?

I've seen it actually. There's a different dimension of anointing that's coming when we have the Bride's revival. It's a different form of revival than we have ever seen before. Brownsville wasn't it. Toronto wasn't it. Even what's going on at Bethel Church is not there yet. There is a different dimension of an anointing that is going to be coming with the Bride's revival, and the Bride will be anointed according to Isaiah 11:2 with the seven spirits of God. That's what we need to understand about former ministers like William Branham, Maria Woodworth-Etter, and Kathryn Kuhlman—these people were prototypes of the Bride. They were forerunners. Every one of them even acknowledged that they lived out of season, or that they were born out of season. They reached over into a future day and pulled something back into their day. John G. Lake actually made that very statement. He knew that he reached over into another dimension, another day. Therefore, we can look at them and know that what they had will identify the coming revival that will be given to the Bride of Christ.

Instead of so many people laying hands on people to impart the power of God, you're going to have the power of the spoken Word doing the work. That's the big difference of what's coming as opposed to what we see now. There is a new realm of authority we will step into. Jesus talked about it with the Roman centurion where the Roman said, "I understand authority and all you have to do is speak the word and my servant will be healed." Jesus marvelled at that faith. That power of the spoken Word will be a big part of what's coming in the days ahead.

Once I asked Paul Cain, "Paul, what was it like when you ministered back in the 1950s and that realm entered the room?" And he said, "One minute you're looking at the people and you see them in the natural, but the next minute it literally looks like a curtain has been opened up, and that whole realm is available to you and you just see everything that's there." That's an entirely different realm of prophetic anointing than what we have right now.

The Lord spoke to me one time when I was really asking for that level of anointing. He said, "Are you really ready to know what people really think about you and still love them anyway?" In other words, in that anointing, there's nothing hidden. Some people said that William Branham, from external appearances, seemed as though he treated his enemies better than he treated his friends. Which means he saw what they really had in their hearts. Often, he was told a day in advance what was going to happen the next day. Paul Cain moved in that. They're really the main two in that last generation that saw that dimension of revelatory power. That's what's coming. That has to be the standard we contend for.

The model for this coming movement is not them, however; it is Samuel. None of his words fell to the ground and he did not beg his bread from the people. Meaning, he had the integrity to never use his gifting for personal gain.

## How do we get there? How do we contend for that?

A.W. Tozer wrote about the issue of character, and he said you have to go to the Lord and insist upon the removal of the stumbling blocks and the issues. So whatever it is, you go to the Lord in humility and say, "You've got to take out the tares in my life." And He'll do that. You know, that's a very answerable prayer.

I think He's refining people, and He's preparing them for that level of anointing. I think it's just a matter of getting positioned with God, and also there has to be a kairos, fullness of time moment, which I personally believe we are approaching. In Isaiah 11:11 the Lord speaks of recovering, for a second time, the remnant of His people. And I believe this anointing will start with a remnant. From there, it will expand and explode.

## Who is the remnant that you're referring to?

I believe they're the overcomers. I think we have to overcome the spirit of the age, which is the Laodicean spirit. I also think we have to overcome our own issues and generational curses and personal agendas. Isaiah 11:13-15 says that if Ephraim will no longer be jealous of Judah, and if Judah will no longer harass Ephraim, then the two of them can come together and go down and plunder the Philistine camp. And so I think that the jealousy and harassing spirits are going to have to be removed from the remnant. And I believe they are. That'd be wonderful to see them removed from the Church! But I'd be happy right now just to see it removed from the remnant, and that is comprised of the overcomers. There is a wheel within the wheel; we have to acknowledge that. We have to acknowledge that there is a remnant within the big company, victorious ones within the midst of that big company. I think the Bride is within the Church but not all the Church is the Bride.

**And so, it's not just a handful of people, or men, who are going to be moving in this anointing, it's a much larger company.**

Oh, it is a much larger company. I believe it's not going to be 1 or 2 as we saw in the last generation, or 10 or 12 even. I do believe it will be hundreds or thousands. I also believe it will be a remnant of the major group of people called the Ecclesia—the Church. People that have actually received the Lord's blood for the remission of their sins; people that have not camped out in Passover, and they have not even camped out in Pentecost, but they have moved on into Tabernacles.

I've been really intrigued with First John 2:27-28 where it talks about destiny and purpose and the anointing teaching us everything we need to know for our destiny. Whenever anyone asks me how to know their destiny, I say go and live the reality of First John 2:27—the anointing which you receive will teach you everything you need to know about your destiny. The next verse says that there is a place to abide in Him so that when He appears we will not shrink away. And so that means there is the ability, at the manifestation of His presence, to withdraw and to be repelled by His coming. That seems kind of odd. But if we're not in the place where we need to be in our character development, when this manifestation comes in, some are going to want to run away.

217

My advice for the next generation is to develop their character and contend for the greater anointing.

Second Timothy says that we have an anointing for our destiny. In other words, we have a sacred destiny. It's one thing to be saved but it's something else altogether to have a divine calling or sacred destiny. And it says that that destiny was set apart for us before the foundation of the world. And so I think right now, the greatest thing we can do is somehow access the grace that was already set apart and pull it down. The Lord showed me that there's a grace hovering over us right now and He said, "The more people you can get to agree to pull it down, the quicker it will come." It is hovering over us right now but it's got to be pulled down into our generation.

**You're not just talking about the revelatory prophetic anointing. You are talking about all the power of the anointing available, whether a person needs healing or anything else, as part of this grace package of anointing that's coming on the Bride.**

Absolutely.

It's the seven spirits of God. If the Bride of Christ will do the works Jesus did, we will have to have the anointing He had. It's one thing to have a word of knowledge, but it's something else to have the Spirit of knowledge. It's one thing to have a word of wisdom, but it's altogether something else to have the Spirit of wisdom. When it says, *"The Spirit of the Lord is upon me"* (KJV), that's the government—the manifestation of His presence—coming in to reside. It produces wisdom and revelation, counsel and might, knowledge and reverential awe. It brings Jehovah Shema—the Lord who is there. If He's there, everything He is comes with Him. I had a very profound vision once where I saw a future meeting, and a person was ministering. Midway through, this ball of light or fire came through the roof, right down next to the minister, and all of a sudden everything started happening simultaneously. The minister was almost like a narrator speaking out what God was doing. He pointed his finger and said, "Over here someone's being healed of cancer. Over here someone's being delivered of drugs." Deliverance and salvation and healings were all taking place simultaneously. This is the anointing that is coming.

I think a new breed's coming in, too. You know, I'd love to see those old anointings restored to anybody who's gotten away from Him for whatever reason. I think this is a season of restoration, no doubt. The new breed will be mingled with it.

I believe that in the future, God will only entrust His anointing raised to the third power to those whom He can trust. The good news is this—if you are reading this, you are being called and qualified. Even if you think you have been disqualified, restoration is imminent. We are all due for an exponential increase. How far do you want to go with Jesus? Do you want the next-generation anointing that is anointing raised to the third power, an anointing where you carry the fullness of the Spirit of power, of love, and of a sound mind?

You don't have to wait for the next outpouring of God in this generation to receive this anointing. The coming outpouring will empower or increase what you are carrying. Until that moment, I encourage you to press into the Lord now, contend for the anointing, and ask Him what area He wants you to focus on in your life. Here is a prayer that will help you prepare for what is to come:

> *Lord, show me how I need to be strengthened in these three equal terms of the anointing of love, power, and a sound mind. Do I need to focus on relationships and develop a heart of love? Do I need to recover from burnout so I stop wanting to run from people and press into Your healing presence and arms of love for awhile so I can carry the next generation of anointing? What areas in my life need cleansing by the blood of Christ? Do I even have a revelation of the cross or do I need to reconnect with who You are and what You have done for me?*

There is time yet to prepare yourself for the future outpouring of God in and through your life and this book will help direct your steps. As you act on what God shows you to do to increase in love and integrity, be encouraged by what the prophets believe is coming—an anointing set apart for you.

If you plan to position yourself to enter into this next-generation anointing, start by taking a look at the foundation of all anointing and reawaken to a greater depth of relationship with Jesus. Along the way, you will discover that love, power, and character development have positioned you for an exponential increase in the anointing. Will you be one who shrinks away when He comes? Or will you be ready to step up and into the fullness of your calling and receive the empowering He releases to fulfill your sacred destiny?

## Endnotes

1. For more information about John Paul Jackson, go to www. streamsministries.com.

2. For more information about Paul Keith Davis, go to www. whitedoveministries.org.

# ABOUT JULIA LOREN

Julia Loren met the Lord while living in Israel and has been a Spirit-filled believer for 33 years (as of the publishing of this book) and in ministry for 21 years. This is her 12th book in print.

Julia Loren is a former journalist and licensed family counselor, who is now a full-time writer, speaker, and prophetic minister. She lives on Camano Island, Washington.

Other books in this series include:

*Shifting Shadows of Supernatural Experiences* (co-authored by James Goll)

*Shifting Shadows of Supernatural Power* (with Bill Johnson, Graham Cooke, and Mahesh Chavda).

You may contact her at juliascribes@yahoo.com
www.julialoren.net

www.divineinterventionbooks.com

# IN THE RIGHT HANDS, THIS BOOK WILL CHANGE LIVES!

Most of the people who need this message will not be looking for this book. To change their lives, you need to put a copy of this book in their hands.

> *But others (seeds) fell into good ground, and brought forth fruit, some a hundred-fold, some sixty-fold, some thirty-fold* (Matthew 13:8).

Our ministry is constantly seeking methods to find the good ground, the people who need this anointed message to change their lives. Will you help us reach these people?

> *Remember this—a farmer who plants only a few seeds will get a small crop. But the one who plants generously will get a generous crop* (2 Corinthians 9:6).

## EXTEND THIS MINISTRY BY SOWING
### 3 BOOKS, 5 BOOKS, 10 BOOKS, OR MORE TODAY,
#### AND BECOME A LIFE CHANGER!

Thank you,

Don Nori Sr., Founder
Destiny Image
Since 1982

# DESTINY IMAGE PUBLISHERS, INC.

*"Promoting Inspired Lives."*

## VISIT OUR NEW SITE HOME AT
## WWW.DESTINYIMAGE.COM

## FREE SUBSCRIPTION TO DI NEWSLETTER

Receive free unpublished articles by top DI authors, exclusive

discounts, and free downloads from our best and newest books.

**Visit www.destinyimage.com to subscribe.**

Write to:     Destiny Image
              P.O. Box 310
              Shippensburg, PA 17257-0310

Call:         1-800-722-6774

Email:        orders@destinyimage.com

For a complete list of our titles or to place an order
online, visit www.destinyimage.com.

FIND US ON FACEBOOK OR FOLLOW US ON TWITTER.

www.facebook.com/destinyimage     facebook
www.twitter.com/destinyimage      twitter